What People Are Saying about *Threshold Bible Study*

"To know and love Jesus and to follow him, we need to know and love the Sacred Scriptures. For many years now, *Threshold Bible Study* has proven to be a vital tool for Catholics seeking to go deeper in their encounter with Christ."
■ **Archbishop José H. Gomez**, *Archbishop of Los Angeles*

"Engagement with the life-changing pedagogy in Stephen Binz's *Threshold Bible Study* brings the understanding that Bible study is a matter of both the mind and heart. Drawing on the finest biblical scholarship, the reader is drawn into individual and group study on themes that deepen one's prayer life and that challenge our call to the Christian discipleship needed for our times."
■ **Antoinette Gutzler, MM**, *former President of the Maryknoll Sisters, former professor at Fu Jen University's St. Robert Bellarmine School of Theology in Taipei, Taiwan*

"In the volumes of his *Threshold Bible Study*, Stephen Binz gives us a rich treasury for nurturing our faith with the power of the biblical word. Besides his fine Bible scholarship, what I like most is the engaging pedagogy that he provides toward group conversation and faith sharing, welcoming the contribution of each participant. While honoring the legacy of the time-tested *lectio divina*, Binz recrafts this soul-engaging process for busy people in our time, encouraging all to reflect and share our faith—the most likely way to grow it."
■ **Thomas Groome**, *Professor of Theology and Religious Education at Boston College*

"*Threshold Bible Study* offers solid scholarship and spiritual depth. It can be counted on for lively individual study and prayer, even while it offers spiritual riches to deepen communal conversation and reflection among the people of God."
■ **Scott Hahn**, *Founder and President, St. Paul Center for Biblical Theology*

"Stephen Binz provides the Church with a tremendous gift and resource in *Threshold Bible Study*. This great series invites readers into the world of Scripture with insight, wisdom, and accessibility. This series will help you fall in love with the Word of God!"
■ **Daniel P. Horan**, *Director of the Center for Spirituality and professor at Saint Mary's College, South Bend*

"*Threshold Bible Study* breaks open the Scriptures and guides readers to a transformation of heart and mind. In this series, Stephen Binz offers his expertise along with his devotion to help Catholics draw nearer to their sacred texts, ponder their rich meaning, and encounter God in a deep, intimate, and sustained way."

■ **Mahri Leonard-Fleckman**, *Professor of Hebrew Bible, College of the Holy Cross*

"*Threshold Bible Study* is appropriately named, for its commentary and study questions bring people to the threshold of the text and invite them in. The questions guide but do not dominate. Stephen Binz's work stands in the tradition of the biblical renewal movement and brings it back to life."

■ **Kathleen M. O'Connor**, *Professor emerita, Columbia Theological Seminary*

"*Threshold Bible Study* is an enriching and enlightening approach to understanding the rich faith which the Scriptures hold for us today. Written in a clear and concise style, *Threshold Bible Study* presents solid contemporary biblical scholarship, offers questions for reflection and/or discussion, and then demonstrates a way to pray from the Scriptures. All these elements work together to offer the reader a wonderful insight into how the sacred texts of our faith can touch our lives in a profound and practical way today. I heartily recommend this series to both individuals and Bible study groups."

■ **Abbot Gregory J. Polan, OSB**, *Conception Abbey, Abbot Primate of the Benedictine Order*

"*Threshold Bible Study* helpfully introduces the lay reader into the life-enhancing process of *lectio divina*, individually or in a group. This series leads the reader from Bible study to personal prayer, community involvement, and active Christian commitment in the world."

■ **Sandra M. Schneiders**, *Professor emerita, Jesuit School of Theology at Santa Clara University*

"The books in the *Threshold Bible Study* series by Stephen J. Binz reflect the ideal Catholic approach to biblical interpretation: sound biblical scholarship; a format accessible for lay readership; and a sensitivity to the Church's life and spirit. This is what the Church means by biblical scholarship at the service of the community of faith."

■ **Donald Senior, CP**, *the late President emeritus of Catholic Theological Union*

"Stephen Binz has put together a great aid for Catholics hungering for Scripture study and application in their daily lives. *Threshold Bible Study* promises to help meet that need."

■ **John Michael Talbot**, *Catholic Christian Recording Artist, Little Portion Hermitage*

THRESHOLD BIBLE STUDY

THE CHURCH'S PRAYERS AT DAWN

Psalms of the Morning

STEPHEN J. BINZ

TWENTY-THIRD PUBLICATIONS
twentythirdpublications.com

TWENTY-THIRD PUBLICATIONS
977 Hartford Turnpike Unit A
Waterford, CT 06385
(860) 437-3012 or (800) 321-0411
www.twentythirdpublications.com

Images: stock.adobe.com

ISBN: 978-1-62785-822-9
Printed in the U.S.A.

bayard

Contents

LESSONS 13–18

LESSONS 19–24

LESSONS 25–30

How to Use *Threshold Bible Study*

Threshold Bible Study is a dynamic, informative, inspiring, and life-changing series that helps you learn about Scripture in a whole new way. Each book will help you explore new dimensions of faith and discover deeper insights for your life as a disciple of Jesus.

The threshold is a place of transition. The threshold of God's word invites you to enter that place where God's truth, goodness, and beauty can shine into your life and fill your mind and heart. Through the Holy Spirit, the threshold becomes holy ground, sacred space, and graced time. God can teach you best at the threshold, because God opens your life to his word and fills you with the Spirit of truth.

With *Threshold Bible Study*, each topic or book of the Bible is approached in a thematic way. You will understand and reflect on the biblical texts through overarching themes derived from biblical theology. Through this method, the study of Scripture will impact your life in a unique way and transform you from within.

These books are designed for maximum flexibility. Each study is presented in a workbook format, with sections for reading, reflecting, writing, discussing, and praying. Each *Threshold* book contains thirty lessons, which you can use for your daily study over the course of a month or which can be divided into six lessons per week, providing a group study of six weekly sessions. These studies are ideal for Bible study groups, small Christian communities, adult faith formation, student groups, Sunday school, neighborhood groups, and family reading, as well as for individual learning.

The commentary that follows each biblical passage launches your reflection on that passage and helps you begin to see its significance within the context of your contemporary experience. The questions following the commentary challenge you to understand the passage more fully and apply it to your own life. Space for writing after each question is ideal for personal study and also allows group participants to prepare for the weekly discussion. The prayer helps conclude your study each day by integrating your learning into your relationship with God.

The method of *Threshold Bible Study* is rooted in the ancient tradition of *lectio divina*, whereby studying the Bible becomes a means of deeper intimacy with God and a transformed life. Reading and interpreting the text (*lectio*) is followed by reflective meditation on its message (*meditatio*). This reading and reflecting flows into prayer from the heart (*oratio* and *contemplatio*). In this way, one listens to God through the Scripture and then responds to God in prayer.

This ancient method assures you that Bible study is a matter of both the mind and the heart. It is not just an intellectual exercise to learn more and be able to discuss the Bible with others. It is, more importantly, a transforming experience. Reflecting on God's word, guided by the Holy Spirit, illumines the mind with wisdom and stirs the heart with zeal.

Following the personal Bible study, *Threshold Bible Study* offers ways to extend personal *lectio divina* into a weekly conversation with others. This communal experience will allow participants to enhance their appreciation of the message and build up a spiritual community (*collatio*). The end result will be to increase not only individual faith but also faithful witness in the context of daily life (*operatio*).

When bringing *Threshold Bible Study* to a church community, try to make every effort to include as many people as possible. Many will want to study on their own; others will want to study with family, a group of friends, or a few work associates; some may want to commit themselves to share insights through a weekly conference call, daily text messaging, or an online social network; and others will want to gather weekly in established small groups.

By encouraging *Threshold Bible Study* and respecting the many ways people desire to make Bible study a regular part of their lives, you will widen the number of people in your church community who study the Bible regularly in whatever way they are able in their busy lives. Simply sign up people at the Sunday services and order bulk quantities for your church. Encourage people to follow the daily study as faithfully as they can. This encouragement can be through Sunday announcements, notices in parish publications, support on the church website, and other creative invitations and motivations.

Through the spiritual disciplines of Scripture reading, study, reflection, conversation, and prayer, *Threshold Bible Study* will help you experience God's grace more abundantly and root your life more deeply in Christ. The risen Jesus said: "Listen! I am standing at the door, knocking; if you hear my voice and open the door, I will come in to you and eat with you, and you with me" (Rev 3:20). Listen to the word of God, open the door, and cross the threshold to an unimaginable dwelling with God!

SUGGESTIONS FOR INDIVIDUAL STUDY

- Make your Bible reading a time of prayer. Ask for God's guidance as you read the Scriptures.
- Try to study daily, or as often as possible according to the circumstances of your life.
- Read the Bible passage carefully, trying to understand both its meaning and its personal application as you read. Some persons find it helpful to read the passage aloud.
- Read the passage in another Bible translation. Each version adds to your understanding of the original text.
- Allow the commentary to help you comprehend and apply the scriptural text. The commentary is only a beginning, not the last word, on the meaning of the passage.
- After reflecting on each question, write out your responses. The very act of writing will help you clarify your thoughts, bring new insights, and amplify your understanding.
- As you reflect on your answers, think about how you can live God's word in the context of your daily life.
- Conclude each daily lesson by reading the prayer and continuing with your own prayer from the heart.
- Make sure your reflections and prayers are matters of both the mind and the heart. A true encounter with God's word is always a transforming experience.
- Choose a word or a phrase from the lesson to carry with you throughout the day as a reminder of your encounter with God's life-changing word.
- For additional insights and affirmation, share your learning experience with at least one other person whom you trust. The ideal way to share learning is in a small group that meets regularly.

SUGGESTIONS FOR GROUP STUDY

- Meet regularly; weekly is ideal. Try to be on time and make attendance a high priority for the sake of the group. The average group meets for about an hour.
- Open each session with a prepared prayer, a song, or a reflection. Find some appropriate way to bring the group from the workaday world into a sacred time of graced sharing.
- If you have not been together before, name tags are very helpful as a group begins to become acquainted with the other group members.
- Spend the first session getting acquainted with one another, reading the Introduction aloud, and discussing the questions that follow.
- Appoint a group facilitator to provide guidance to the discussion. The role of facilitator may rotate among members each week. The facilitator simply keeps the discussion on track; each person shares responsibility for the group. There is no need for the facilitator to be a trained teacher.
- Try to study the six lessons on your own during the week. When you have done your own reflection and written your own answers, you will be better prepared to discuss the six scriptural lessons with the group. If you have not had an opportunity to study the passages during the week, meet with the group anyway to share support and insights.
- Participate in the discussion as much as you are able, offering your thoughts, insights, feelings, and decisions. You learn by sharing with others the fruits of your study.
- Be careful not to dominate the discussion. It is important that everyone in the group be offered an equal opportunity to share the results of their work. Try to link what you say to the comments of others so that the group remains on the topic.
- When discussing your own personal thoughts or feelings, use "I" language. Be as personal and honest as appropriate and be very cautious about giving advice to others.

- Listen attentively to the other members of the group so as to learn from their insights. The words of the Bible affect each person in a different way, so a group provides a wealth of understanding for each member.
- Don't fear silence. Silence in a group is as important as silence in personal study. It allows individuals time to listen to the voice of God's Spirit and the opportunity to form their thoughts before they speak.
- Solicit several responses for each question. The thoughts of different people will build on the answers of others and will lead to deeper insights for all.
- Don't fear controversy. Differences of opinions are a sign of a healthy and honest group. If you cannot resolve an issue, continue on, agreeing to disagree. There is probably some truth in each viewpoint.
- Discuss the questions that seem most important for the group. There is no need to cover all the questions in the group session.
- Realize that some questions about the Bible cannot be resolved, even by experts. Don't get stuck on some issue for which there are no clear answers.
- Whatever is said in the group is said in confidence and should be regarded as such.
- Pray as a group in whatever way feels comfortable. Pray for the members of your group throughout the week.

Schedule for Group Study

Session 1: Introduction — Date: ____________________

Session 2: Lessons 1–6 — Date: ____________________

Session 3: Lessons 7–12 — Date: ____________________

Session 4: Lessons 13–18 — Date: ____________________

Session 5: Lessons 19–24 — Date: ____________________

Session 6: Lessons 25–30 — Date: ____________________

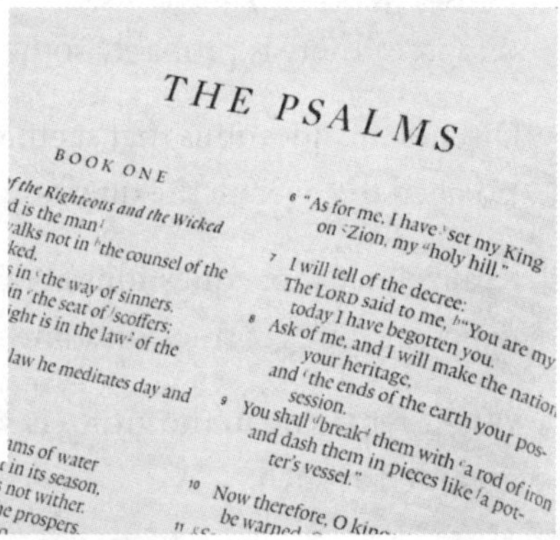
THE PSALMS
BOOK ONE
"As for me, I have set my King
on Zion, my holy hill."
I will tell of the decree:
The LORD said to me, "You are my
today I have begotten you.
Ask of me, and I will make the nation
your heritage,
and the ends of the earth your pos-
session.
You shall break them with a rod of iron
and dash them in pieces like a pot-
ter's vessel."
Now therefore, O king
be warned.

Awake, my soul! Awake, O harp and lyre! I will awake the dawn.
I will give thanks to you, O Lord, among the peoples;
I will sing praises to you among the nations. PSALM 57:8–9

The Church's Prayers at Dawn

Dawn is the time when the world begins to grow light after the night, the time when everything is still tranquil and hushed, before things get stirring. It's the time before the kids get up, before the phone begins ringing, when even the pets are still asleep. The break of day is the time when the people of God begin to pray. The Lord longs to speak to us in the morning quiet: "Be still, and know that I am God!" (Ps 46:10).

Do you awake the day or does the day awake you? The singer of the psalms declares, "Awake, O harp and lyre! I will awake the dawn" (Pss 57:8; 108:2). The psalmist wants to wake up early to seize the day, beating the day to the punch, meeting it by chanting psalms, reflecting on Scripture, and voicing prayer. The faithful one desires that praise of God be the first words on his lips.

The Jewish tradition recommends prayer upon rising each morning. The writer of the book of Wisdom prays, "One must rise before the sun to give you thanks, and must pray to you at the dawning of the light" (Wis 16:28). Jesus himself rose early to have time to pray to the Father: "In the morning, while it was still very dark, he got up and went out to a deserted place, and there he prayed" (Mark 1:35). Likewise, the early Christians began their prayer in the morning hours. In the monastic tradition, the monks cultivated a period of great silence from the last prayer at night to the morning prayer, so that the first words spoken in the new day would be praise to God.

St. Basil the Great, the fourth-century bishop in Cappadocia, describes how prayer at dawn is intended to sanctify the morning: "[Prayer] is said in the morning in order that the first stirrings of our mind and will may be consecrated to God and that we may take nothing in hand until we have been gladdened by the thought of God … or set our bodies to any task before we do what has been said: 'Lord, in the morning you hear my voice; in the morning I plead my case to you, and watch' (Ps 5:3)." Keeping watch is the proper way to begin the day. When the sun rises, it shines on the believer already at prayer.

The Psalms of the Morning are those psalms traditionally chosen for the church's Lauds, or Morning Prayer. The motif that predominates in these psalms is the praise of God, often with a mention of the sunrise, waking at the break of day, or divine light. The first gleam of dawn calls to mind that Christ is the true Light, that he comes to dispel the world's darkness and reign over it.

It was at dawn that Christ rose from the tomb, victorious over the darkness of sin and death. It is his resurrection that gives the fullest meaning to the church's morning praise. The first gleam of dawn recalls to our minds that Christ is the true Light, that he comes to dispel spiritual darkness and reign over the world. There is no sleeping when the new age is dawning.

Rising early to pray may at first be sheer discipline, but as we commit to it each day, it begins to shift into delight. As it was with David and then with Jesus, morning prayer becomes a joyful encounter with the Lord. Before we hear the outside noises, we tune in and listen for the word of God. Awakening early to seek God offers us a head start on all the ensuing activity of the day and approaches the day from this sacred place of readiness.

Reflection and discussion

- When was the last time I rose before the sun?

- Why would praise of God seem to be the predominant mood of morning prayer?

The Prayerbook of Israel, Jesus, and the Church

The psalms have been described as the prayerbook of the people of God. While many prayers can be found throughout the books of the Bible, Psalms is the only book made up entirely of prayers. While we pray the psalms, we are praying with and in Israel, Jesus, and the church, and all three have something to teach us about prayer. While the psalms are two to three thousand years old, they are amazingly contemporary. They have been prayed by the kings and priests of Israel, the apostles of the church, and the whole community of God's people in the temple, synagogue, monastery, cathedral, chapel, and home.

Praying the psalms with and in the people of Israel means being in solidarity with our ancestors in faith, taking on their longings and sharing in the relationship that God initiated with them. There are several aspects of prayer that we learn from praying the psalms in solidarity with the people of Israel. First, we realize that prayer is concrete. The psalms do not lend themselves to sweeping generalizations but focus on specific matters and the concrete circumstances of life. Second, we see that prayer is filled with emotion. Passion, hurt, rage, anger, hatred—all of these are expressed openly to God. The words of the psalms are not censored or filtered through more pious language. Because the psalms deal with human emotion in a candid way, they are honest, genuine, and healing.

Third, in praying the psalms with Israel, we learn that the prayer of Israel is focused on Torah. The teachings of God, expressed in the first five books of the Bible, are not vague, romantic, or subjective. The Torah centers on the ethical content of faith and tells God's people that the primary way of being faithful to God is listening with obedience. Fourth, we recognize that prayer is centered on Jerusalem. Zeal for Jerusalem, for Zion, is the focusing desire for all of Israel's life. All the yearnings of Israel's faith tradition are embodied in Jerusalem—the city of peace, the site of the temple, the place of the Messiah.

Fifth, in praying the psalms with Israel, we realize that prayer is directed toward justice. God's vision of a just society and a just people fills Israel's prayer. Israel prays to a God who has compassion on the poor, the needy, the broken in spirit. The righteous person is one who practices God's vision of justice, and the one who does evil to others is opposed to God's will and sets himself on the way that leads to ruin. Sixth, we see that prayer is filled with hope. Hoping for something new from God is the constant prayer of Israel. God is not at all predictable; and because the people of God know that, they know with confidence that something will happen when they pray that won't happen if they don't pray. Elie Weisel, a survivor of the Holocaust, said that what makes a Jew a Jew is his inability to quit hoping. The people of Israel "keep on" no matter what happens because they trust their future to God.

This prayerbook of the temple is also the prayerbook of Jesus. Jesus prayed the prayers of his people every day. He sang the psalms at every Jewish feast. He learned them in his home and in the synagogue at Nazareth. He prayed them with his whole heart and soul, and he probably knew many of them by heart. The psalms helped form Jesus' relationship with the Father, and Jesus began to understand who he was called to be by praying the psalms. The prayers and teachings of Jesus throughout the gospels echo the psalms.

Jesus shared human life in all its fullness, with its pain and distress, its joys and hopes. He knew all human experience from the inside. He thrilled with the realization of God's presence, and he suffered the anguish of God's apparent absence and seeming indifference to suffering and injustice. He knew what it was like to be ill-treated and rejected. Jesus was the fullest voice of Israel. He embodied all of Israel's history and all of her future. He was the true prophet, priest, and king. He was the suffering servant, the innocent victim, the poor man whose voice is heard throughout the psalms.

As Christians, we pray the psalms with Jesus. The psalms take on a new and unique intensity when read in him. Each psalm has been written an octave higher because it has passed through the life, death, and resurrection of Jesus. Each psalm is intensified because it has passed through the heart and mind and lips of Jesus. By making the prayers of Jesus our own prayers, we enter into the same world of meaning that shaped Jesus' self-understanding. When we pray in him, we take on his mind, his heart, his way of relating to the Father. The psalms, for us, are a primary way of seeking what Paul says is the goal of Christian life: "It is no longer I who live, but it is Christ who lives in me" (Gal 2:20).

Because the psalms are the prayers of Jesus, they have become the prayerbook of the church. The early disciples continued the prayer of its Jewish roots—chanting the psalms and listening to Scripture. Through much of the church's history, the daily chanting of the psalms was part of a Christian's daily life. The monastic office was prayed by monks and nuns, and the cathedral office was prayed by the clergy and lay people. Twice a day, for morning and evening prayer, the people of God would gather in the churches to pray the Liturgy of the Hours.

Today, we have the opportunity to reclaim the psalms of our faith tradition. The liturgy of our church, in the Eucharist and the Liturgy of the Hours, encourages the whole church to pray the psalms. When we pray a psalm of lament and we don't feel particularly sorrowful, we realize that other members of the church are lamenting and we pray with them. When we pray a hymn of thanksgiving and we don't feel particularly grateful ourselves, we can realize that the people of God has much to be thankful about. Praying the psalms with the church helps us realize that we are the body of Christ at prayer. When one member suffers, the whole body suffers; when one member rejoices, we all have reason to be glad.

When we pray in Christ, we are never praying alone. When we go into our room and close the door to pray, we always pray as part of the people of God; we pray with the church, the body of Christ. We are a people who find our identity and purpose within the community of faith. Because the psalms come from a people who experienced God in community, they widen our vision and enlarge our hearts to include others.

Reflection and discussion

- What does it mean to me to know that the psalms are the prayerbook of Jesus?

- What characteristics of the psalms help me to realize that I never pray alone?

The Psalms as a School for Prayer

Although the psalms are, of course, not the only way to pray or even the most perfect or correct way to pray, the wonderful thing about them is that they teach us to pray better. They do not replace our spontaneous, personal prayer, but they extend the range of our prayer and model for us a variety of ways to relate to God. They offer us new viewpoints from which to pray, give us new images with which to relate to God, and expand our vocabulary of prayer.

The psalms express prayers that are generally much wider in range and richer in content than the sometimes narrow range and limited content we allow ourselves in prayer. The psalms convince us that there are many ways to pray, many ways to describe God, and many ways to live in relationship with God.

The psalms teach us to pray from our lived experiences, assuring us that all the occurrences of life, both extraordinary and very ordinary, are appropriate to bring to conversation with God. When we pray the psalms, we reflect on the experiences of the psalmist and bring our own life into the prayer, allowing these two realities to interact and illuminate one another. The words the psalmist addresses to God are bold, eloquent, and passionate, and we bring our own free reflections on our lives. Prayer arises when we let our minds and hearts move back and forth between the Scriptural words of the psalms and the prayerful words that arise from our own life experiences. The words of the psalms bring energy, form, and authority to what we discover about ourselves; and conversely, our experiences bring to the words of the psalms a vitality and immediacy that must always be reasserted within God's living word.

St. Ambrose of Milan wrote about the psalms in these words:

> What is more pleasing than a psalm? David expresses it well: Praise the Lord, for a song of praise is good: let there be praise of our God with gladness and grace. Yes, a psalm is a blessing on the lips of the people, a hymn in praise of God, the assembly's homage, a general acclamation, a word that speaks for all, the voice of the church, a confession of faith in song. It is the voice of complete assent, the joy of freedom, a cry of happiness, the echo of gladness. It soothes the temper, distracts from care, lightens the burden of sorrow. It is a source of security at night, a lesson in wisdom by day. It is a shield when we are afraid, a celebration of holiness, a vision of serenity, a promise of peace and harmony. It is like a lyre, evoking harmony from a blend of notes. Day begins to the music of a psalm. Day closes to the echo of a psalm.

Who would not want to add these spiritual treasures to their day? Imagine the richness that would enter the fabric of our daily prayer if we began to pray the psalms.

The foundation of biblical faith is the speaking of God to his people. God's word goes forth, and it is natural that we should speak back—in praise, thanksgiving, trust, frustration, or confusion. The psalms display this conversational quality of faith and are the privileged way that we speak and respond to God who has spoken to us. The motto taken by St. John Henry Newman when he became a Cardinal was *cor ad cor loquitur* (heart speaks to heart). There is no better description of what happens when we pray the psalms. To the God who has poured out his heart to us, we pour out our own hearts.

Reflection and discussion

- What would I like the psalms to teach me so that I can pray better?

- Why are the psalms described as a dialogue between the divine and human hearts?

Beginning to Study and Pray the Psalms

As we study the Psalms of the Morning during the coming weeks, make these ancient prayers your own. Allow them to resonate with your own personal situation, your temperament, your joys and sorrows, your worries, responsibilities, and hopes for the future. Pray them aloud, allowing the mood of each psalm to determine the tone in which you read them. Mark words and phrases that speak powerfully to you, and memorize verses to recall throughout the day. Let the psalms lead you into your own prayer from the heart.

Don't worry about understanding every line of every psalm. The word of good translators and commentators helps, but some parts of these ancient texts baffle even scholars. An example of these perplexing aspects of the psalms is the word "Selah," which you will find occasionally between lines of the psalms. Some believe that this word marks a transition in the text, like a change of speaker or a shift in tone. Others say it indicates a place to pause, perhaps to emphasize a point or invite readers to a moment of reflection. Could it be a musical marker, indicating a pause for a musical interlude? No one really knows. The meaning of "Selah" has been lost in antiquity.

The desert monks of the early Christian centuries taught a fruitful method for praying the psalms. They would slowly, reflectively recite the psalm, then they would pause for an extended time of silent prayer. So, they prayed with the psalm, then they let the psalm be the spark and inspiration for their own personal prayer. Likewise, our own prayers become richer and fuller because they have been formed and animated and enlivened by the word of God. The psalms show us how to break out of whatever limits we have placed on our relationship with God. We can bring our whole self to prayer—our body, mind, feelings, imagination, intuition, and gestures. We can be totally honest and bold with God, unrestrained, with nothing to hide.

St. Augustine describes what occurred when he was in church as the psalms were being sung: "How I wept when I heard your hymns and canticles, being deeply moved by the sweet singing of your church. Those voices flowed into my ears, truth filtered into my heart, and from my heart surged waves of devotion. Tears ran down, and I was happy in my tears." Who of us would not desire this blessing? Let us use the psalms to love God more deeply, the truest romance and the greatest adventure.

Reflection and discussion

- Why is silence important when learning to pray the psalms?

- What does it mean to bring one's whole self to prayer?

Prayer

Lord, please be with me throughout this day and help me navigate whatever comes my way. I ask that you guide my thoughts, words, and actions, and, most importantly, help me to reflect and live out my life in a way that honors you. Prepare my mind and heart to study these sacred psalms so that I may better know you and love you. Direct my reading and meditation so that it leads me to prayer and witness, contributing ever more fully to Christ's reign on earth as in heaven. Keep me faithful during these weeks to the challenges that your word offers to me.

SUGGESTIONS FOR FACILITATORS, GROUP SESSION 1

1. If the group is meeting for the first time, or if there are newcomers joining the group, it is helpful to provide name tags.

2. Distribute the books to the members of the group.

3. You may want to ask the participants to introduce themselves and tell the group a bit about themselves.

4. Ask one or more of these introductory questions:
    - What drew you to join this group?
    - What is your biggest fear in beginning this Bible study?
    - How is beginning this study like a "threshold" for you?

5. You may want to pray this prayer as a group:
   Come upon us, Holy Spirit, to enlighten and guide us as we begin this study of the Psalms of the Morning. You inspired the authors of Scripture to reveal your presence throughout the history of salvation. This inspired word has the power to convert our hearts and change our lives. Fill our hearts with desire, trust, and confidence as you shine the light of your truth within us. Motivate us to read the Scriptures and give us a deeper love for God's word each day. Bless us during this session and throughout the coming week with the fire of your love.

6. Read the Introduction aloud, pausing at each question for discussion. Group members may wish to write down the insights of the group as each question is discussed. Encourage several members of the group to respond to each question.

7. Don't feel compelled to finish the complete Introduction during the session. It is better to allow sufficient time to talk about the questions raised than to rush to the end. Group members may read any remaining sections on their own after the group meeting.

8. Instruct group members to read the first six lessons on their own during the six days before the next group meeting. They should write out their own answers to the questions as preparation for next week's group discussion.

9. Fill in the date for each group meeting under "Schedule for Group Study."

10. Conclude by praying aloud together the prayer at the end of the Introduction.

O Lord, in the morning you hear my voice; in the morning I plead my case to you, and watch. PSALM 5:3

In the Morning You Hear My Voice

PSALM 5

1 *Give ear to my words, O Lord;*
give heed to my sighing.
2 *Listen to the sound of my cry,*
my King and my God,
for to you I pray.
3 *O Lord, in the morning you hear my voice;*
in the morning I plead my case to you, and watch.

4 *For you are not a God who delights in wickedness;*
evil will not sojourn with you.
5 *The boastful will not stand before your eyes;*
you hate all evildoers.
6 *You destroy those who speak lies;*
the Lord abhors the bloodthirsty and deceitful.

7 *But I, through the abundance of your steadfast love,*
will enter your house,
I will bow down toward your holy temple
in awe of you.
8 *Lead me, O Lord, in your righteousness*
because of my enemies;
make your way straight before me.

9 *For there is no truth in their mouths;*
their hearts are destruction;
their throats are open graves;
they flatter with their tongues.
10 *Make them bear their guilt, O God;*
let them fall by their own counsels;
because of their many transgressions cast them out,
for they have rebelled against you.

11 *But let all who take refuge in you rejoice;*
let them ever sing for joy.
Spread your protection over them,
so that those who love your name may exult in you.
12 *For you bless the righteous, O Lord;*
you cover them with favor as with a shield.

The psalmist prays to God in the morning hours, beginning with a threefold plea: "give ear to my words," "give heed to my sighing," "listen to the sound of my cry" (verses 1–2). Prayer can be offered in traditional words, in sighs too deep for words, or in an anguished cry for help. The prayer is audible speech or chant, not merely written words or inner meditation. The language is highly personal and relational, addressed to God as the divine Lord, "my King," and "my God." The psalmist prays at daybreak, rising early to both "plead" to God in prayer and "watch" with confident expectation (verse 3). The psalm became a traditional morning prayer because it sets the tone for how to begin a prayerful day.

The psalm's five stanzas alternate between the petitioner who pleads before the Lord (verses 1–3, 7–8, 11–12) and who seeks protection from God against the wicked (verses 4–6, 9–10). This concentric structure highlights the third stanza as the theological center of the psalm (verses 7–8). Here the supplicant expresses assurance that he will enter the divine presence, finding safe passage to the "house" of God. God's "holy temple" is the place of communion and intimacy with God. The Lord himself will take his faithful one by the hand and lead him through the streets of the city, making his "way straight." The morning prayers in the temple will provide the psalmist the interior grace to face an often hostile world. The psalmist's serene confidence is rooted in two qualities of God: the abundance of God's "steadfast love" (*hesed*, in Hebrew) and his "righteousness" (*sedaqah*, in Hebrew). Both of these terms, referring to the Lord's faithful mercy and his saving justice, are terms used throughout the Scriptures to express the solidarity of God with his people in the bonds of covenant.

Surrounding this central stanza focusing on the temple, the second and fourth stanzas describe the "wickedness" that besieges the psalmist and the "evil" that God casts from his presence. These doers of wickedness are described as boastful, evildoers, liars, bloodthirsty, and deceitful (verses 5–6). The divine opposition to them is stated in the strongest terms: God "hates," "destroys," and "abhors" them. Their evil conduct consists in malicious speech, designated by the mouth, heart, throat, and tongue (verse 9). Their mouths are full of falsehood, their hearts plot deceit, their throats are open tombs, and their seductive tongues provide a slippery chasm leading to death. While the psalmist pleads for God to "make them bear their guilt," their retribution is decidedly of their own making (verse 10). Evil recoils on its perpetrators. The wicked become their own victims, and their punishment will be in like measure to their crimes.

The psalms demonstrate the power of human speech. Spoken words have the ability to destroy people, or, when speech is used in prayer, it can safeguard life. The psalm moves from pleading prayer in the midst of enemies to confident expectation that those who "take refuge" in God will "rejoice," "sing for joy," and "exult" in God (verse 11). God will spread divine "protection" over those who long for God's holy temple, for God's dwelling among his people. The psalmist seeks God's protection not only from wicked enemies but also from becoming like them. The "righteous" are those who love God, trust in him, and want to be led in his ways.

Reflection and discussion

- What does this psalm teach me about how to begin my mornings?

- Where is God's holy temple where I can seek the divine presence?

- How is human speech used to cause anguish for others? How can it be put to better use?

Prayer

Faithful and merciful Lord, who covers the righteous with your shield, spread your protection over me and help me to love your name. Strengthen me to walk in righteousness and do what is just.

What are human beings that you are mindful of them, mortals that you care for them? Yet you have made them a little lower than God, and crowned them with glory and honor. PSALM 8:4–5

God's Majesty and Humanity's Dignity

PSALM 8

1*O Lord, our Sovereign,*
how majestic is your name in all the earth!

You have set your glory above the heavens.
2*Out of the mouths of babes and infants*
you have founded a bulwark because of your foes,
to silence the enemy and the avenger.

3*When I look at your heavens, the work of your fingers,*
the moon and the stars that you have established;
4*what are human beings that you are mindful of them,*
mortals that you care for them?

5*Yet you have made them a little lower than God,*
and crowned them with glory and honor.
6*You have given them dominion over the works of your hands;*
you have put all things under their feet,
7*all sheep and oxen,*
and also the beasts of the field,
8*the birds of the air, and the fish of the sea,*
whatever passes along the paths of the seas.

9 *O Lord, our Sovereign,*
how majestic is your name in all the earth!

This hymn of praise celebrates who God is and what God has done, all in a spirit of awe and wonder. It is addressed wholly to God, beginning and ending with an exclamation of God's sovereign rule over the cosmos (verses 1, 9). God's supreme majesty is evident in all creation, and our rightful response is to cry out in praise and worship. The acclaim of even powerless infants confounds God's enemy and avenger, believing themselves too self-sufficient to submit to God (verse 2).

Gazing at the moon and the stars, the vastness of the night sky can lead us to a feeling of insignificance (verse 3). With poetic imagery, the psalmist describes God's arrangement of the heavenly bodies as the work of God's "fingers," the handiwork of the divine artisan. Within such a magnificent creation, the singer asks, "What are human beings that you are mindful of them, mortals that you care for them?" (verse 4). Who are we in relation to the grandeur of the heavens or the majesty of God? Communal worship of our transcendent God offers us a healthy dose of humility in the face of the awesome wonder of creation.

Though small and insignificant from the standpoint of human rationality, from the view of God's revelation human beings have a special and unique place in the order of creation. In God's plan our value is incomparable. We have been made "a little lower than God" (verse 5), placed between God and his other creatures, as stewards of creation. In fact, human beings have been given a share in God's royal rule, "crowned" with honor and glory, the regal traits of God. Though minuscule in comparison to the Creator and his wondrous works, earthly mortals are appointed to represent God's reign to other creatures.

This divinely appointed task for humanity to serve as God's royal regents in the world is described as "dominion" over the works of God's hands (verse 6). Humans are endowed by God with tremendous dignity and remarkable responsibility in regard to the other creatures of the world. The sphere of this dominion is over all living creatures, both domesticated and wild animals (verse 7) as well as the birds of the air and the fish of the sea (verse 8). Yet, human authority over creation is far from absolute. It is a power exercised only at the behest of the Sovereign, a control that must reflect the purposes of the Creator. Dominion is nothing less than representing the reign of God in the world.

Reflection and discussion

- How does this psalm of praise challenge me to think about my dignity and accountability as God's viceroy in the world?

- In what ways has humanity misunderstood its dominion over creation and replaced it with domination of the earth?

- What natural experiences serve as reminders to me of God's sovereign majesty?

Prayer

Sovereign Lord, when I look at the vast beauty of your creation, I marvel at the dignity and responsibility you have given to me. May I give glory to you by all I say and do.

In the heavens he has set a tent for the sun, which comes out like a bridegroom from his wedding canopy, and like a strong man runs its course with joy. PSALM 19:4–5

Creation and the Torah Announce God's Glory

PSALM 19

1 *The heavens are telling the glory of God;*
and the firmament proclaims his handiwork.
2 *Day to day pours forth speech,*
and night to night declares knowledge.
3 *There is no speech, nor are there words;*
their voice is not heard;
4 *yet their voice goes out through all the earth,*
and their words to the end of the world.

In the heavens he has set a tent for the sun,
5 *which comes out like a bridegroom from his wedding canopy,*
and like a strong man runs its course with joy.
6 *Its rising is from the end of the heavens,*
and its circuit to the end of them;
and nothing is hid from its heat.

7 *The law of the Lord is perfect,*
reviving the soul;
the decrees of the Lord are sure,
making wise the simple;

8 *the precepts of the Lord are right,*
rejoicing the heart;
the commandment of the Lord is clear,
enlightening the eyes;
9 *the fear of the Lord is pure,*
enduring forever;
the ordinances of the Lord are true
and righteous altogether.
10 *More to be desired are they than gold,*
even much fine gold;
sweeter also than honey,
and drippings of the honeycomb.

11 *Moreover by them is your servant warned;*
in keeping them there is great reward.
12 *But who can detect their errors?*
Clear me from hidden faults.
13 *Keep back your servant also from the insolent;*
do not let them have dominion over me.
Then I shall be blameless,
and innocent of great transgression.

14 *Let the words of my mouth and the meditation of my heart*
be acceptable to you,
O Lord, my rock and my redeemer.

This two-part psalm describes the two ways that God is revealed to us: through creation (verses 1–6) and through Scripture (verses 7–14). God has given us these two means through which to know him and experience his glory. Although these two sections may have originally been two separate poems, they have been thoughtfully unified through the concept of "word" or "speech." In the first section, the inaudible words of nature give praise to God; in the second section, the audible words of the Torah instruct humanity.

As the psalm opens, the sky's expanse speaks of God's glory and creative artistry (verse 1). By day, the firmament "pours forth speech," and by night it "declares knowledge" (verse 2). Each line of the opening stanza expresses a word normally associated with verbal communication: tell, proclaim, speech, declare, words, and voice. Although the wonders of creation reveal God and give praise to God, "their voice" is inaudible to humanity (verse 3). Although the language of creation goes out to the furthest parts of the world (verse 4), it does so without speech or words.

The next stanza describes a radiant sunrise bursting forth on the horizon (verses 5–6). We wonder at the persistent daily journey the sun makes across the sky. At dawn the sun shines forth from its tent of nightly rest, like a bridegroom or warrior ready to run the path ahead of him. The sun travels from one end of the sky to the other, distributing its heat to warm the earth. This poetic description of the sun suggests that what the sun is to the natural world, Scripture is to the rational being. As the sun gives light and warmth to the world, God's will expressed in the Torah gives life to the human spirit. The sun's rays penetrate the invisible depths of the earth's terrain; likewise, the divine law reaches the innermost regions of the human conscience.

With a sudden transition, the psalm then describes the way God is revealed to us through Scripture. The tone and style significantly shift. The first part of the psalm uses the generic term for "God" (*El*, in Hebrew), and his revelation is mysterious, elusive, and inaudible. In this second part, God's personal name, "the Lord," is associated with his communication, which is verbal and explicit (verses 7–9). This section consists of six synonyms for the Torah, the teachings of God to his people Israel: the "law of the Lord," the "decrees of the Lord," the "precepts of the Lord," the "commandment of the Lord," the "fear of the Lord," and the "ordinances of the Lord." These six descriptions are each followed by an attribute of God's instructions. They are characterized by perfection, surety, rightness, clarity, purity, and truth. Those who follow God's teachings will produce lives that are distinguished by these qualities.

The Torah is not a collection of oppressive regulations and threatening prohibitions. It expresses God's loving will for human life. A life of obedience to God's law will deliver a life of joy, maturity, wisdom, and blessing. The Torah is more desirable than the finest gold and more satisfying than the sweet "drippings of the honeycomb" (verse 10).

In light of the inaudible words of creation and the clear words of the Lord's Torah, the poet concludes the psalm with sincere words of prayer.

This cosmic vision of God's glory and the divine will prompt the psalmist to seek pardon even from unintended errors and "hidden faults" (verse 12). Because insolent people scorn God's will, the poet prays to be protected from the arrogant so that he may be "blameless and innocent of great transgression" (verse 13). The sky's quiet beauty, the sun's penetrating rays, and the splendor of God's law reach the innermost depths of the poet's heart. So, the psalm concludes with the poet's desire that these words and meditations be acceptable to the Lord and represent a life lived in harmony with God.

Reflection and discussion

- In what ways are creation and Scripture like two books that reveal the nature and will of God?

- In what ways can superficiality obscure my spiritual vision?

- How is the order, beauty, and hope I find in the natural world a foretaste of that found in the word of God?

Prayer

O Lord, my rock and my redeemer, may I meditate on your word day and night so that I experience the order, beauty, and hope you offer me. Help me to listen carefully to your voice in both creation and Scripture.

Lift up your heads, O gates! and be lifted up, O ancient doors! that the King of glory may come in. PSALM 24:7

The King of Glory Enters His Temple

PSALM 24

[1]*The earth is the Lord's and all that is in it,*
the world, and those who live in it;
[2]*for he has founded it on the seas,*
and established it on the rivers.

[3]*Who shall ascend the hill of the Lord?*
And who shall stand in his holy place?
[4]*Those who have clean hands and pure hearts,*
who do not lift up their souls to what is false,
and do not swear deceitfully.
[5]*They will receive blessing from the Lord,*
and vindication from the God of their salvation.
[6]*Such is the company of those who seek him,*
who seek the face of the God of Jacob. Selah

[7]*Lift up your heads, O gates!*
and be lifted up, O ancient doors!
that the King of glory may come in.
[8]*Who is the King of glory?*
The Lord, strong and mighty,
the Lord, mighty in battle.

9*Lift up your heads, O gates!*
and be lifted up, O ancient doors!
that the King of glory may come in.
10*Who is this King of glory?*
The Lord of hosts,
he is the King of glory. Selah

The occasion of the psalm is the Lord's victory procession entering the temple. The liturgy begins with the proclamation of God's victory over all the forces of chaos and destruction (verses 1–2). Next, the question is asked and answered: Who is qualified to join the procession and enter the gates of the temple with the Lord (verses 3–6)? Finally, the procession arrives at the temple and a dialogue ensues between those in the procession and the gatekeepers (verses 7–10). The proclamation of the Lord's titles becomes the signal to open the ancient doors of God's dwelling place.

The pilgrimage seems to commemorate David's bringing up the ark of the covenant to Jerusalem. The ark, the living symbol of God's presence with his people, was brought to the city by David and later, when the temple was built by Solomon, was brought into the sanctuary. On occasion, the ark was taken out of the temple to lead Israel in battle over its enemies and then solemnly transported back to the sanctuary. The pilgrimage depicted here is a victory procession celebrating God's kingship.

As in other ancient Near Eastern literature, God's creation is described here as the victory of a divine warrior over the forces of chaos, represented by the seas and rivers (verse 1–2). According to the ancient understanding, God established the world and all that it contains above the unruly waters. Because God has vanquished the rivers and seas, the divine warrior is declared the divine king over all the earth. This victory shout alerts us to the fact that God owns the world and reigns over it. But the order of creation is not a given; rather, the Lord must continually exert his divine power to maintain it against the continually threatening powers of chaos.

Who are the people with whom God shares this victory, those who may ascend the temple mount and enter the sacred precincts (verse 3)? They are the ones who are aligned with God and reflect his character. In this entrance liturgy, the questions are followed by a formal list of the qualifications for entry. The list includes two positive character traits: "those who have clean hands and pure hearts" (verse 4). The first is related to blameless behavior and the second to honorable motives. These positive traits are followed by two negative actions: "who do not lift up their souls to what is false, and do not swear deceitfully"; that is, those who refuse to give honor to idols so as to replace allegiance to God and those who reject telling lies so as to deceive others.

This list of conditions for entry is followed by God's pledge to give the people "blessing" and "vindication," the gift of abundant life and pardon from offenses (verse 5). These promises indicate that the qualifications for entry do not express moral perfection. Rather, the procession includes all those "who seek" God, those who desire association with God and are willing to conform their behavior and motives to the divine will (verse 6). Making a pilgrimage to God's temple is an external expression of one's internal desire to seek "the face of the God of Jacob." The liturgical procession consists of those joined in covenant with God and longing to encounter the Lord in worship.

As the liturgical dialogue continues, we hear the voices of those in the procession as they approach the temple gates and the gatekeepers. The throng requests that the entrance of the temple be opened: "Lift up your heads, O gates! and be lifted up, O ancient doors! that the King of glory may come in" (verse 7). The questioning reply of the gatekeepers implies that this title for God is unknown to them: "Who is the King of glory?" (verse 8).

The first response to this inquiry signals that Israel's divine King is a mighty hero in battle. When the dialogue is repeated for dramatic effect, the response again associates the King of Glory with "the Lord of hosts," the leader of the heavenly army (verses 9–10). The hero of Israel's battles is also their glorious King, the God of Jacob, and the God of salvation.

Reflection and discussion

- What lines of this psalm indicate a liturgical procession?

- What behaviors might be represented by “clean hands”? What motives might be represented by “pure hearts”?

- If God is a military hero as well as a glorious king, what are today’s battles that God and his people must fight against?

- What new insights do I attain when I pray this psalm with the understanding that Christ is the King of glory, who won the battle against sin at his passion and now ascends to his place in heaven?

Prayer

King of Glory, who conquers chaos and leads God’s people in battle, come to my assistance as I am confronted by the power of evil and the temptations of sin. Keep my hands clean and my heart pure so that I may enter the gates of your kingdom.

The Lord sits enthroned over the flood; the Lord sits enthroned as king forever. May the Lord give strength to his people! May the Lord bless his people with peace! PSALM 29:10–11

The Sevenfold Voice of the Lord

PSALM 29

1 *Ascribe to the Lord, O heavenly beings,*
ascribe to the Lord glory and strength.
2 *Ascribe to the Lord the glory of his name;*
worship the Lord in holy splendor.

3 *The voice of the Lord is over the waters;*
the God of glory thunders,
the Lord, over mighty waters.
4 *The voice of the Lord is powerful;*
the voice of the Lord is full of majesty.

5 *The voice of the Lord breaks the cedars;*
the Lord breaks the cedars of Lebanon.
6 *He makes Lebanon skip like a calf,*
and Sirion like a young wild ox.

7 *The voice of the Lord flashes forth flames of fire.*
8 *The voice of the Lord shakes the wilderness;*
the Lord shakes the wilderness of Kadesh.

9 *The voice of the Lord causes the oaks to whirl,*
and strips the forest bare;
and in his temple all say, "Glory!"

[10]The Lord sits enthroned over the flood;
the Lord sits enthroned as king forever.
[11]May the Lord give strength to his people!
May the Lord bless his people with peace!

In this psalm of praise, the "heavenly beings," all the angels and holy ones, are invited to honor the Lord along with God's people (verse 1). The work resembles Canaanite poetry, in which the heavenly beings represent the pantheon of gods ruled by the senior god Baal, the god of the thunderstorm. Although the psalm was perhaps influenced by Canaanite literature, it is here a hymn to the Lord of all. The prayer urges all to "ascribe" honor to the Lord, that is, to bestow on God alone whatever "glory and strength" we might consider our own. We must avoid ascribing glory and strength to any other religious or political entity besides the Lord. To his name alone belongs glory, and he alone may be worshiped "in holy splendor" (verse 2).

The main body of the psalm describes God's majesty reflected in a furious thunderstorm. In fact, the Hebrew word used most often in the psalm is *qol,* pronounced with the full glottal shock of the letter "q." The word mimics the sound of thunder and means "voice" (verses 3–5, 7–9). The expression "the voice of the Lord" is uttered a total of seven times, and in the psalm's original language conveys the expression of a repeated thunder roll.

The storm is generated over the "waters" of the sea, the chaotic powers that continue to manifest themselves in disruptions of the earth. The booming voice of God moves with terrifying majesty. The powerful storm breaks the majestic cedars, causes the mountains of Lebanon and Sirion to leap like young, frightened animals, and even shakes the wilderness. The wind and rain swish the landscape, while the lightning bolts flash forth in "flames of fire," stripping the forest bare. This is certainly a psalm to be prayed aloud, allowing its words to rumble, invoking astonishment and awe.

As a hymn of praise, a doxology (literally, an expression of glory), one of the key terms of the psalm is "glory." The Lord is given the title "the God of glory," a variant of "the King of Glory" (Ps 24:7–10). At the end of the manifestation of God in the storm, all in the temple shout "Glory!" The divine glory is the summary of God's attributes, the display of God's strength, power, splendor, and majesty in the world.

Although most of the psalm is energetic and loud, it ends with an image of God serene on his throne (verse 10). The still point is God. Although the Lord's thunderous voice has manifested his power, he now sits enthroned above the flood, reigning over the forces of chaos as "king forever." The entire psalm featured the natural world: mountain heights, empty wilderness, trees, and wild animals. But the final prayer requests that God give "strength" to his people and bless them with "peace" (verse 11). There is nothing for God's people to fear.

Reflection and discussion

- What do I see, hear, and feel when witnessing a thunderstorm?

- What other events of life evoke expressions of astonishment, wonder, and praise within me?

- If this psalm is inspired by a Canaanite poem honoring the god Baal, what does this tell me about the similarities between the ancient religions of Canaan and Israel?

Prayer

Lord and Creator, whose voice sounds throughout the earth, how great thou art! Calm the storms that beset my heart and bless your people with peace. To you be glory and praise, now and forever.

Our soul waits for the Lord; he is our help and shield. Our heart is glad in him, because we trust in his holy name. PSALM 33:20–21

Waiting for the Lord with Hope

PSALM 33

1*Rejoice in the Lord, O you righteous.*
Praise befits the upright.
2*Praise the Lord with the lyre;*
make melody to him with the harp of ten strings.
3*Sing to him a new song;*
play skillfully on the strings, with loud shouts.

4*For the word of the Lord is upright,*
and all his work is done in faithfulness.
5*He loves righteousness and justice;*
the earth is full of the steadfast love of the Lord.

6*By the word of the Lord the heavens were made,*
and all their host by the breath of his mouth.
7*He gathered the waters of the sea as in a bottle;*
he put the deeps in storehouses.

8*Let all the earth fear the Lord;*
let all the inhabitants of the world stand in awe of him.
9*For he spoke, and it came to be;*
he commanded, and it stood firm.

10*The Lord brings the counsel of the nations to nothing;*
he frustrates the plans of the peoples.

11 *The counsel of the Lord stands forever,*
the thoughts of his heart to all generations.
12 *Happy is the nation whose God is the Lord,*
the people whom he has chosen as his heritage.

13 *The Lord looks down from heaven;*
he sees all humankind.
14 *From where he sits enthroned he watches*
all the inhabitants of the earth—
15 *he who fashions the hearts of them all,*
and observes all their deeds.
16 *A king is not saved by his great army;*
a warrior is not delivered by his great strength.
17 *The war horse is a vain hope for victory,*
and by its great might it cannot save.

18 *Truly the eye of the Lord is on those who fear him,*
on those who hope in his steadfast love,
19 *to deliver their soul from death,*
and to keep them alive in famine.

20 *Our soul waits for the Lord;*
he is our help and shield.
21 *Our heart is glad in him,*
because we trust in his holy name.
22 *Let your steadfast love, O Lord, be upon us,*
even as we hope in you.

This hymn of praise opens with imperatives, inviting the liturgical assembly to "rejoice in the Lord," "praise the Lord," "sing to him," and "play skillfully" on instruments to the Lord (verses 1–3). Those who are righteous and upright are urged to join in with singing, shouting, and melodic instruments to give joyful praise to God. The psalm is described as "a new song" because God's renewing actions as creator, sovereign, and deliverer are forever new.

The next stanza expresses the reasons for the praise of God (verses 4–5). These five terms are those that describe the way of the Lord most often in the

Bible: upright, faithfulness, righteousness, justice, and steadfast love. This terminology is applied to both the "word" and the "work" of God. These manifestations of the Lord go together; the work is accomplished by the word. As the hymn continues, it teaches the assembly to hope in God by describing the Lord as the only one in whom we can place our trust.

The central body of the hymn describes the spheres over which the Lord rules, beginning with the created world (verses 6–9). "By the word of the Lord the heavens were made," as the creation account of Genesis also suggests. God spoke and the world came to be. To God's word is added "the breath of his mouth," God's dynamic power. The creation of the heavens and earth involves the containment of the chaotic waters, which, in the ancient worldview, are stored above the heavens and under the land, all of which can overwhelm the earth with floods. God's confinement of these watery forces with the sky and the land is no more challenging than filling a "bottle" or putting the floodwaters in "storehouses." So, earth's inhabitants must revere and "stand in awe" of God's authority. The Lord speaks and things happen; God commands and the world stands firmly ordered.

In addition to God's rule over creation, his rule extends to nations and peoples (verses 10–12). "The counsel of the nations," those plans and designs that express the nations' goals, stands in contrast with "the counsel of the Lord," which expresses God's ideals and lasting plan. The former is temporary and passing, while the latter "stands forever" for "all generations." The nation "whose God is the Lord" is ancient Israel, the people God chose not because of any merit of their own but to serve as an example to the world of what a covenant relationship with the Lord is like. They are "happy" because they have a mission to bring God's blessing to all the nations.

God's ongoing care for "all humankind" is emphasizes through four verbs that speak of God's visual connection with "all the inhabitants of the earth": God "looks down," "sees," "watches," and "observes" (verses 13–15). The one who cares intimately for all people is also the one who "fashions the hearts of them all," implying the ability to look into their hearts and see the interior motives and desires of each person. With God, there is no isolation or secrecy because the lives of all are ever present to him.

Because of such personal concern for his people, God is completely trustworthy. A "great army" cannot save a king; "great strength" cannot save a warrior; the "great might" of a war horse cannot save one who hopes for victory (verses

16–17). These are ineffective means for delivering a person from lasting harm. The only source of real salvation is God's commitment to humanity, expressed by that divine eye watching from heaven (verses 18–19). The key to God's deliverance, then, is not in accumulating weapons and instruments of human power. It is found in "fear" of the Lord, that is, reverent submission to God in all things; and in "hope in his steadfast love," that is, waiting in confident expectation for God to act on our behalf. This creative tension between reverence for God and trust in his promises, obedience in the present and confidence in the future, establishes in us a longing to conform our desires with God's desires.

Because God is "our help and shield," we can "wait" with patience for him, be "glad" for his watchful care, and "trust in his holy name" (verses 20–21). In closing, the only verse voiced directly to God, the psalmist transforms his conviction into a prayer (verse 22). It asks neither for victory nor even for strength but only for God's unfailing love. The singer asks that God's "steadfast love" be upon us as we hope in the Lord.

Reflection and discussion

- How does the power of God manifested in creation move me to worship?

- What does the psalm have to say to today's world of immense military power?

Prayer

Lord of heaven and earth, of all peoples and nations, look down from your throne and see the hearts of your people. Help us to entrust our plans and our future to you as we hope in your promises.

SUGGESTIONS FOR FACILITATORS, GROUP SESSION 2

1. If there are newcomers who were not present for the first group session, introduce them now.

2. You may want to pray this prayer as a group:
   Lord of heaven and earth, when we see the rising sun and gaze upon the magnificence of your creation, we know we can hope in your promises and entrust our plans and our future to you. May we listen carefully as you reveal your glory in both creation and Scripture, so that we may experience the wisdom, beauty, and hope you want to share with us. Strengthen us to walk in righteousness and give you glory by all we say and do. Spread your protective shield over your people, calm the storms that beset our hearts, and bless us with your peace.

3. Ask one or both of the following questions:
   - What was your biggest challenge in Bible study over this past week?
   - What did you learn about yourself this week?

4. Discuss lessons 1 through 6 together. Assuming that group members have read the Scripture and commentary during the week, there is no need to read it aloud. As you review each lesson, you might want to briefly summarize the Scripture passages of each lesson and ask the group what stands out most clearly from the commentary.

5. Choose one or more of the questions for reflection and discussion from each lesson to talk over as a group. You may want to ask group members which question was most challenging or helpful to them as you review each lesson.

6. Keep the discussion moving, but don't rush it in order to complete more questions. Allow time for the questions that provoke the most discussion.

7. Instruct group members to complete lessons 7 through 12 on their own during the six days before the next group meeting. They should write out their own answers to the questions as preparation for next week's group discussion.

8. Conclude by praying aloud together the prayer at the end of lesson 6 or any other prayer you choose.

How precious is your steadfast love, O God! All people may take refuge in the shadow of your wings. They feast on the abundance of your house, and you give them drink from the river of your delights. PSALM 36:7–8

The Ways of the Wicked and the Ways of the Lord

PSALM 36

1 *Transgression speaks to the wicked*
deep in their hearts;
there is no fear of God
before their eyes.
2 *For they flatter themselves in their own eyes*
that their iniquity cannot be found out and hated.
3 *The words of their mouths are mischief and deceit;*
they have ceased to act wisely and do good.
4 *They plot mischief while on their beds;*
they are set on a way that is not good;
they do not reject evil.

5 *Your steadfast love, O Lord, extends to the heavens,*
your faithfulness to the clouds.
6 *Your righteousness is like the mighty mountains,*
your judgments are like the great deep;
you save humans and animals alike, O Lord.

7 *How precious is your steadfast love, O God!*
All people may take refuge in the shadow of your wings.
8 *They feast on the abundance of your house,*
and you give them drink from the river of your delights.

9 *For with you is the fountain of life;*
in your light we see light.

10 *O continue your steadfast love to those who know you,*
and your salvation to the upright of heart!
11 *Do not let the foot of the arrogant tread on me,*
or the hand of the wicked drive me away.
12 *There the evildoers lie prostrate;*
they are thrust down, unable to rise.

The first section of this prayer describes the stance of those who are wicked. Their malice is shown to be caused not just by human weakness but by human rebellion against God (verses 1–4). People do not simply fall into evil; it arises from deep in their hearts and is cultivated by their own strategies. Because they lack a proper "fear of God," they flatter themselves and willfully deceive themselves that "their iniquity cannot be found out," opposed, and denounced. From the heart and intentions of the wicked ones, their sinfulness moves to the words of their mouths. Their speech is filled with "mischief and deceit," calculated to do harm to others. They have turned their backs on the ways of wisdom and goodness, substituting these virtues with shrewdness and cunning. So consumed are the wicked with their own schemes and selfish desires that they do not even sleep at night. They plot harm in their beds, then they leave home to implement their evil plans. This is a psychologically brilliant description of the wicked from the inside out, from their innermost thoughts to their words to their deeds.

Then, without any transition, the psalmist begins addressing God (verses 5–6). Amid the presence of evil, the singer perceives the more ultimate and enduring reality of God. The first two attributes of God, "steadfast love" and "faithfulness," serve as a marvelous summary of God's character. The next two divine attributes, "righteousness" and "judgments," effectively summarize God's will for the world. The creative composition of these verses, moving in descending order from the heavens to the clouds to the mountains to the great depth of the sea, affirms that God's character and the divine will permeate the whole of creation. From the heights to the depths, there is no place where God's saving love is ineffective. In between, where living creatures flourish, God's saving love desires a flourishing life for "humans and animals alike."

Continuing to address God, the psalmist praises God's faithful and constant love. Amid the destructive effects of the wicked one, God offers a safe alternative: "All people may take refuge in the shadow of your wings" (verse 7). But God is not only a tender protector but also a generous host. God's people enjoy a rich banquet in God's presence and drink from his river of abundant life (verse 8). God is not only transcendent in the heavens but also close to his people, providing for their fragile human needs. The images of life and light express our human dependence on God, the source of all (verse 9). Life—as abundance, community, and restoration—is the gift of the Lord. Light—as the presence of God that scatters the darkness of evil—enables us to see the world anew and experience God's saving presence.

The final stanza is a petition to God requesting that those who know God and whose hearts are upright in confessing their dependence on him continue experiencing his "steadfast love" rather than the power of the wicked (verses 10–12). In the face of all the threatening shapes that evil takes, this prayer renews our understanding that our lives are God's gift and are protected by his grace. Although the psalmist is threatened with being stomped on with "the foot of the arrogant" and shoved away by "the hand of the wicked," the evildoers are ultimately cast down, unable to rise. Those who plead for God to deliver them may trust that God is doing so.

Reflection and discussion

- How do I experience wickedness moving from the inside out, from thoughts, to words, to deeds?

- Which sentence of the psalm will help me best contemplate God's steadfast love?

Prayer

Lord our God, let the light of your face shine upon me and the shadow of your wings give me shelter. Help me to recognize the abundant gifts that issue from your generous grace and protect me from the snares of evil.

O send out your light and your truth; let them lead me; let them bring me to your holy hill and to your dwelling. PSALM 43:3

Holy Longing for God's Presence

PSALM 42

1*As a deer longs for flowing streams,*
so my soul longs for you, O God.
2*My soul thirsts for God,*
for the living God.
When shall I come and behold
the face of God?
3*My tears have been my food day and night,*
while people say to me continually, "Where is your God?"

4*These things I remember,*
as I pour out my soul:
how I went with the throng,
and led them in procession to the house of God,
with glad shouts and songs of thanksgiving,
a multitude keeping festival.
5*Why are you cast down, O my soul,*
and why are you disquieted within me?
Hope in God; for I shall again praise him,
my help 6*and my God.*

My soul is cast down within me;
therefore I remember you

from the land of Jordan and of Hermon,
from Mount Mizar.
7 *Deep calls to deep*
at the thunder of your cataracts;
all your waves and your billows
have gone over me.
8 *By day the Lord commands his steadfast love,*
and at night his song is with me,
a prayer to the God of my life.

9 *I say to God, my rock,*
"Why have you forgotten me?
Why must I walk about mournfully
because the enemy oppresses me?"
10 *As with a deadly wound in my body,*
my adversaries taunt me,
while they say to me continually,
"Where is your God?"

11 *Why are you cast down, O my soul,*
and why are you disquieted within me?
Hope in God; for I shall again praise him,
my help and my God.

PSALM 43

1 *Vindicate me, O God, and defend my cause*
against an ungodly people;
from those who are deceitful and unjust
deliver me!
2 *For you are the God in whom I take refuge;*
why have you cast me off?
Why must I walk about mournfully
because of the oppression of the enemy?

3 *O send out your light and your truth;*
let them lead me;

let them bring me to your holy hill
and to your dwelling.
4*Then I will go to the altar of God,*
to God my exceeding joy;
and I will praise you with the harp,
O God, my God.

5*Why are you cast down, O my soul,*
and why are you disquieted within me?
Hope in God; for I shall again praise him,
my help and my God.

The psalm opens with the stunning image of a deer searching desperately for flowing streams in the wilderness (42:1). The distressing picture indicates that the thirsty animal cannot find water in the parched land. Likewise, the psalmist is longing for the presence of God, the only experience that can slake the thirsty soul (42:2). With this poignant image, the psalmist claims that the object of our most fervent yearning is God. The presence of the living God is our deepest desire. The soul cannot survive without God. The thirst for God drives the pilgrimage of faith, and that longing can drive us to despairing frustration as well as to joyful fulfillment.

The psalmist asks, "When shall I come and behold the face of God?" Fortunately, the psalmist understands what is missing. The reason for his discontent is the absence of an encounter with God. He longs for the tangible experience of God's presence remembered from his past. But now, the longing for flowing streams is expressed by flowing tears, streaming down his face day and night (42:3). His thirst is intensified by grief. While the psalmist asks "when" he will encounter God, the mocking question "Where is your God?" pierces his heart. The psalmist's oppressors seek to convince him that God has forgotten him or cast him away. When, where, and especially "why"—these are the questions of the struggling soul throughout the psalm.

The psalmist's hope is sustained by memory of times past, when traveling in procession to the house of God, the temple in Zion (42:4). There, in the holy city of Jerusalem, he would join with God's people in the pilgrimage festivals. United with the multitude of Israelites approaching the altar in the appointed liturgies, shouting praises to God and chanting songs of thanksgiving, the psalmist would experience the Lord's presence. Here, in this sacred space, in sacramental worship, the soul can "behold the face of God."

The dynamics of the psalmist's prayer for help are especially evident in the refrain in which the psalmist speaks to his own soul (42:5; 42:11; 43:5). Questions about the source of his distress, "why" God seems so painfully absent, gives way to "hope in God," the anticipation of better days to come, when he is able to again praise God and trust in his help. The threefold repetition of this refrain indicates that Psalms 42 and 43 were originally regarded as one psalm. The combined psalms, then, fall into three equal parts: the first two parts, in Psalm 42, describe the psalmist's predicament, while the third part, in Psalm 43, forms the psalmist's cry to God for help.

In the second part of the prayer, the psalmist continues to reflect on his alienation from God's presence in the storm of suffering (42:6–8). It seems that he is either literally or imaginatively in the far north of Israel, near Mount Hermon, the snow-covered peak from which flows the sources of the Jordan River. Here, amid the thundering waterfalls, the psalmist is overwhelmed with a deluge of grief, yet God's might rings clear. "Deep calls to deep," as the deep anguish of the psalmist meets the deep power of God. As the violent waves continue to sweep over him, God strengthens him and saturates his parched soul. Throughout his experience of God's absence, he never doubts God's faithfulness. Because he has intimately experienced God's loving presence in the past, he trusts in God's steadfast love by day and sings a prayer to God by night.

Pleading to God, "my rock," the psalmist continues to ask, "Why?" (42:9). His adversaries continue their taunt: "Where is your God?" (42:10). Again, in the refrain, the "why" of God's absence gives way to the psalmist's reservoir of hope (42:11).

Psalm 43 forms the final part of this prayer for help, as the psalmist appeals to God with more conviction. He describes his foes as ungodly, deceitful, and unjust, pleading for rescue from them (43:1). Though his "why" questions remain, he confidently seeks refuge in God (43:2). He asks God to send out his "light" and "truth" as guides to lead him back to the temple, the "holy hill" where God dwells (43:3). There he will "go to the altar of God," and there he will give God praise with musical accompaniment (43:4).

In a prayer that complains of divine absence, God is present throughout, mentioned in nearly every line, including titles that suggest an ongoing relationship: the living God, the face of God, my help and my God, the God of my life, my rock, the God in whom I take refuge, and my exceeding joy. The pain of separation from God seems to become a way of feeling the presence. The distance may be real, or perhaps the poet is employing geographical images to express his state of mind. Likewise, the assaults of the jeering enemies may be physical, or they may be projections of the poet's inner darkness and doubts. Because the prayer contains no explicit details of the poet's situation, it may be prayed by anyone who feels separated from God and longing for God's presence. It charts the extremes of joy and despair, divine presence and absence, hope and despair, flood and drought, alternating repeatedly in a never-resolved conversation, testifying that the journey of faith is not a relaxed stroll but a challenging pilgrimage.

Reflection and discussion

- Why is it impossible for the soul to survive without experiencing the presence of God? What keeps me spiritually hydrated during the dry seasons of life?

- Which lines of the psalm express the current state of my journey of faith?

Prayer

God our help in ages past, may my memory of your presence sustain my hope for the future. In the anguish of my longing for you, send me your light and your truth to guide me to the place of your dwelling.

Sing praises to God, sing praises; sing praises to our King, sing praises.
For God is the king of all the earth; sing praises with a psalm.
PSALM 47:6–7

God Reigns as King on Mount Zion

PSALM 47

1 *Clap your hands, all you peoples;*
shout to God with loud songs of joy.
2 *For the Lord, the Most High, is awesome,*
a great king over all the earth.
3 *He subdued peoples under us,*
and nations under our feet.
4 *He chose our heritage for us,*
the pride of Jacob whom he loves. Selah

5 *God has gone up with a shout,*
the Lord with the sound of a trumpet.
6 *Sing praises to God, sing praises;*
sing praises to our King, sing praises.
7 *For God is the king of all the earth;*
sing praises with a psalm.

8 *God is king over the nations;*
God sits on his holy throne.
9 *The princes of the peoples gather*
as the people of the God of Abraham.
For the shields of the earth belong to God;
he is highly exalted.

PSALM 48

1 *Great is the Lord and greatly to be praised*
in the city of our God.
His holy mountain, 2 *beautiful in elevation,*
is the joy of all the earth,
Mount Zion, in the far north,
the city of the great King.
3 *Within its citadels God*
has shown himself a sure defense.

4 *Then the kings assembled,*
they came on together.
5 *As soon as they saw it, they were astounded;*
they were in panic, they took to flight;
6 *trembling took hold of them there,*
pains as of a woman in labor,
7 *as when an east wind shatters*
the ships of Tarshish.
8 *As we have heard, so have we seen*
in the city of the Lord of hosts,
in the city of our God,
which God establishes forever. Selah

9 *We ponder your steadfast love, O God,*
in the midst of your temple.
10 *Your name, O God, like your praise,*
reaches to the ends of the earth.
Your right hand is filled with victory.
11 *Let Mount Zion be glad,*
let the towns of Judah rejoice
because of your judgments.

12 *Walk about Zion, go all around it,*
count its towers,
13 *consider well its ramparts;*
go through its citadels,

that you may tell the next generation
[14]that this is God,
our God forever and ever.
He will be our guide forever.

Psalm 47 is a hymn that praises God as the king over all the earth. It begins with the call to worship, consisting of two imperatives: "Clap your hands" and "shout to God" (47:1). What follows are the reasons why God is deserving of praise: he is the awesome Lord, the Most High, king over all the earth; he subdued peoples and nations; and he chose to enter into covenant with Israel, "the pride of Jacob" (47:2–4). Although God is king over all peoples, he has selected a special people for his own possession, to bind them to himself in faithful love.

The occasion for this psalm, however, is not just general praise of God but rather a liturgical drama. The Lord has "gone up" while the trumpet (*shofar*, in Hebrew) sounds (47:5). The ark of the covenant, understood as the throne of God's presence on earth, is carried in procession up to the temple, perhaps during an annual festival or victory parade. The congregation is invited to "sing praises," the imperative repeated five times (47:6–7). There follows again the reasons why God is deserving of such exuberant praise: the Lord is "king over the nations" and "sits on his holy throne" (47:8). In the temple of Jerusalem, God is envisioned as enthroned on the ark of the covenant, as he is revered by all the nations. He is honored by the "princes of the peoples," the leaders of other nations who are gathered with God's own heritage, "the people of the God of Abraham" (47:9). God alone is exalted over the nations, for "the shields of the earth," all the symbols of power and rule, belong to God.

Although the original historic occasion of the psalm was God's enthronement in Jerusalem's temple, the psalm continued to be sung long after the ark was lost and the temple destroyed. Through this hymn of praise, especially when it is sung in the liturgy of God's people, the past memory and meaning is actualized in the present experience. The celebration of the reign of God involves past memory, present experience, and future hope. God's kingdom becomes present in the liturgical moment, but it is never fully there. God's people always long for future fulfillment while expressing the joy of God's universal rule.

Psalm 48 praises Jerusalem with exalted titles and extravagant tribute. The relatively small city in the ancient Middle East is called "the city of our God" (48:1). The ridge on which Jerusalem sits is called Mount Zion, "beautiful in elevation." The Jebusite city that David conquered is called "city of the great King" (48:2). This unimposing capital of Israel is called "joy of all the earth." The vocabulary does not correspond to the material and political reality of Jerusalem. Rather, the poet is expressing the transcendent dimensions of the earthly city. The song envisions the earthly in terms of the heavenly, the temporal in terms of the eternal. No claim can be too extravagant for the holy city of God.

Jerusalem is a visible witness to the invisible presence of God. The approach to God's purportedly invincible city inspired fright in its enemies and pride in its pilgrims. The invading kings were astounded and panicked, trembling like a woman in labor and shattered as by a storm that smashes cargo ships (48:4–7). But the pilgrims saw for themselves what they had always heard about God's city (48:8). They pondered God's faithful love and praised God's name for his judgments (48:9–11).

The song ends with a call to the pilgrims to make a procession that circles the city (48:12). Its architectural features—its towers, ramparts, and citadels—express the mighty and protective qualities of God. The city is God's visible witness. It provides the pilgrims with memories to tell "the next generation" about God (48:13–14). Since God's reign is symbolized by the physical plan of Jerusalem, people can know and respond to God through his city. Jerusalem is a visible sign of God's commitment to his people. The pilgrims can return to their homes and speak about Zion in such a way that others will know better who God is and what God has in store for his people's future.

Reflection and discussion

- Why are God's people invited to clap their hands, shout for joy, and sing praises to God?

- What enabled the poet to endow the modest physical qualities of Jerusalem with such transcendent characteristics?

- What do I want to tell "the next generation" about my experience with God?

Prayer

Great King of all the nations, your name and your praise reach to the ends of the earth. As I ponder your steadfast love and remember Zion, help me to trust that you have great things in store for the future.

Create in me a clean heart, O God, and put a new and right spirit within me. Do not cast me away from your presence, and do not take your holy spirit from me. PSALM 51:10–11

Offering God a Broken and Contrite Heart

PSALM 51

1*Have mercy on me, O God,*
according to your steadfast love;
according to your abundant mercy
blot out my transgressions.
2*Wash me thoroughly from my iniquity,*
and cleanse me from my sin.

3*For I know my transgressions,*
and my sin is ever before me.
4*Against you, you alone, have I sinned,*
and done what is evil in your sight,
so that you are justified in your sentence
and blameless when you pass judgment.
5*Indeed, I was born guilty,*
a sinner when my mother conceived me.

6*You desire truth in the inward being;*
therefore teach me wisdom in my secret heart.
7*Purge me with hyssop, and I shall be clean;*
wash me, and I shall be whiter than snow.

[8]Let me hear joy and gladness;
let the bones that you have crushed rejoice.
[9]Hide your face from my sins,
and blot out all my iniquities.

[10]Create in me a clean heart, O God,
and put a new and right spirit within me.
[11]Do not cast me away from your presence,
and do not take your holy spirit from me.
[12]Restore to me the joy of your salvation,
and sustain in me a willing spirit.

[13]Then I will teach transgressors your ways,
and sinners will return to you.
[14]Deliver me from bloodshed, O God,
O God of my salvation,
and my tongue will sing aloud of your deliverance.

[15]O Lord, open my lips,
and my mouth will declare your praise.
[16]For you have no delight in sacrifice;
if I were to give a burnt offering, you would not be pleased.
[17]The sacrifice acceptable to God is a broken spirit;
a broken and contrite heart, O God, you will not despise.

[18]Do good to Zion in your good pleasure;
rebuild the walls of Jerusalem,
[19]then you will delight in right sacrifices,
in burnt offerings and whole burnt offerings;
then bulls will be offered on your altar.

Although it might seem at first that this psalm is dominated by the vocabulary of sin, in reality it is saturated with the vocabulary of God's grace. The opening offers several synonyms for wrongdoing: transgressions, iniquity, and sin (verses 1–2). Yet, these same verses use several metaphors to describe the process of forgiveness: blotting out, thorough washing, and cleansing from sin. Through these words and images, the psalmist humbly acknowledges his wrong and pleads for God's mercy.

The penitent is unable to conceal his sin from God; indeed, it causes him great distress: "For I know my transgressions, and my sin is ever before me" (verse 3). His sin stares him in the face. Because he has encountered the living God, like so many other characters in Scripture, he is painfully aware of his own sinfulness and unworthiness to come into God's holy presence.

The psalmist acknowledges that our being is disordered and prone to sin (verses 4–5). From conception and birth, every person is immersed in the sin of humanity. So, the problem is not just the need to be pardoned from a particular wrong but to be delivered from the predicament of my being. God's will as the criterion for human acts reveals wrongdoing to be not only an offense against other people but a sin against God. For this reason, all of God's judgments and verdicts are thoroughly just.

Despite the bad news about the human situation, the psalm is about the good news of God's mercy, grace, and love. Sin does not have the last word in the psalm, and it will not have the final word in the human situation. The following verses consist of requests for cleansing and forgiveness. The psalmist knows that his renewal will not come just from his own efforts to change but from God working deep within him. He prays, "You desire truth in the inward being; therefore teach me wisdom in my secret heart" (verse 6). Rather than a change of situation, the psalmist knows that he needs an inner transformation. He prays that he may be re-created: "Create in me a clean heart, O God, and put a new and right spirit within me" (verse 10). In the Bible, "create" is an act that can be done only by God. What is said of the "heart" and "spirit" characterizes the condition and direction of a person's life. A clean heart and a right spirit designate a mind and will oriented to God, true to God's covenant, and ready to offer praise.

The psalmist's vocabulary of forgiveness and re-creation is the ritual language of worship: purging with hyssop and washing with water (verse 7). They are external actions that express an inward transformation. Yet, it is not the action itself, the sacrifice or burnt offering, that pleases God (verses 16–17). Rather, the contrite spirit and broken heart, which the sacrifice symbolically represents, is the offering that God accepts. The humble heart and spirit designate the mind and will turned to God, knowing that they belong to God and offering themselves to God.

The restoration of the city of Jerusalem (verses 18–19) completes the transformation of God's people. Both the restored city and the renewed people are the result of God's forgiveness. In the transformed Jerusalem, inhabited by a people with clean hearts and right spirits, the ritual worship of God can resume in a way that is in harmony with God's designs. The continual chanting of this psalm from repentant hearts expresses the praise of a joyful and forgiven people.

The penitent has become the teacher of other transgressors and sinners (verse 13). He teaches us, through this psalm, to acknowledge our sins because only then can we recognize God's merciful grace. And if we don't acknowledge God's grace, we fail to appreciate who God is and how God operates in the world.

Reflection and discussion

- What do I most appreciate about how this psalm demonstrates the psychological and spiritual dynamics of sin and forgiveness?

- Why do people only understand the reality and significance of their sin through a personal encounter with God?

Prayer

Have mercy on me, O God, and cleanse me from my sin. Create in me a clean heart and right spirit that I may offer you a living sacrifice, live in your covenant, and give you praise.

My heart is steadfast, O God, my heart is steadfast.
I will sing and make melody. Awake, my soul! Awake, O harp and lyre!
I will awake the dawn. PSALM 57:7–8

Singing Praises to Awake the Dawn

PSALM 57

1*Be merciful to me, O God, be merciful to me,*
for in you my soul takes refuge;
in the shadow of your wings I will take refuge,
until the destroying storms pass by.
2*I cry to God Most High,*
to God who fulfills his purpose for me.
3*He will send from heaven and save me,*
he will put to shame those who trample on me. Selah
God will send forth his steadfast love and his faithfulness.

4*I lie down among lions*
that greedily devour human prey;
their teeth are spears and arrows,
their tongues sharp swords.

5*Be exalted, O God, above the heavens.*
Let your glory be over all the earth.

6*They set a net for my steps;*
my soul was bowed down.
They dug a pit in my path,
but they have fallen into it themselves. Selah

7 My heart is steadfast, O God,
my heart is steadfast.
I will sing and make melody.
8 Awake, my soul!
Awake, O harp and lyre!
I will awake the dawn.
9 I will give thanks to you, O Lord, among the peoples;
I will sing praises to you among the nations.
10 For your steadfast love is as high as the heavens;
your faithfulness extends to the clouds.

11 Be exalted, O God, above the heavens.
Let your glory be over all the earth.

Beginning with a twice-repeated plea, "Be merciful to me," the psalmist expresses confidence that God will provide refuge from danger (verses 1–3). Seeking refuge in the shadow of God's wings suggests the image of the protective wings of an eagle guarding its nestlings from the destructive storm. The shadow of God's wings also suggests the wings of the cherubim above the ark of the covenant. Through this symbol, God's people perceived a unity between God's earthly and heavenly presence. The psalmist is confident that God will send forth his twin attributes, "steadfast love" and "faithfulness," those two divine qualities that have sustained God's people in covenant in every generation.

The poet describes his dangerous condition with images of a hunt. The attackers are like lions (verse 4). With spears and arrows for fangs and sharp swords for tongues, they seek to devour their prey with false accusation and abusive speech. The poet then becomes a hunted animal (verse 6). Its trappers lay the net and dig a pit in hopes of catching the prey. Yet, with both images, the one who trusts God can be confident. He can confidently "lie down among lions," and his assailants are bound to fall into their own trap. Such are the ways of God's protective care.

After a night of steadfast prayer, the psalmist declares himself ready before the sun rises for a new day (verses 7–8). He summons his soul, his musical instruments, and a voice filled with song, and he declares, "Awake, my soul!

Awake, O harp and lyre! I will awake the dawn." All are ready to participate in the song of thanksgiving and praise to God.

The psalm is a proclamation to the peoples and nations that God is a reliable refuge for his people (verses 9–10). For the "steadfast love" and the "faithfulness" of God extend high into the heavens. The dawn of every new day is a time to turn again to God with confidence. Whatever destructive storms God's people may face, we can take heart that God is the unfailing source of salvation for those who turn to him. The refrain, "Be exalted, O God, above the heavens… Let your glory be over all the earth," prays that God's glory may shine out throughout the cosmos (verses 5, 11).

The psalm moves from the plea of an individual for God's protection to a proclamation of God's international and universal saving will. The needs of the individual are presented within the wider context of God glory. The psalm also moves from night to day, from nightmarish storms, wild animals, and weapons of war to grateful praise.

Reflection and discussion

- When have I been glad to awake in the morning from a nightmare? Which verse of the psalm would express my gratitude upon awakening?

- Rather than reluctantly falling into each new day, how can I "awake the dawn"?

Prayer

God Most High, who fulfills your purpose for me, send forth your steadfast love and your faithfulness to give me confidence. May your glory be exalted above the heavens and over all the earth.

**Because your steadfast love is better than life,
my lips will praise you. So I will bless you as long as I live;
I will lift up my hands and call on your name.** PSALM 63:3–4

The Desire to Give Worship to God

PSALM 63

1 *O God, you are my God, I seek you,*
my soul thirsts for you;
my flesh faints for you,
as in a dry and weary land where there is no water.
2 *So I have looked upon you in the sanctuary,*
beholding your power and glory.
3 *Because your steadfast love is better than life,*
my lips will praise you.
4 *So I will bless you as long as I live;*
I will lift up my hands and call on your name.

5 *My soul is satisfied as with a rich feast,*
and my mouth praises you with joyful lips
6 *when I think of you on my bed,*
and meditate on you in the watches of the night;
7 *for you have been my help,*
and in the shadow of your wings I sing for joy.
8 *My soul clings to you;*
your right hand upholds me.

9 *But those who seek to destroy my life*
shall go down into the depths of the earth;
10 *they shall be given over to the power of the sword,*
they shall be prey for jackals.
11 *But the king shall rejoice in God;*
all who swear by him shall exult,
for the mouths of liars will be stopped.

The psalm expresses intense longing for God. The yearning is physical, emotional, and spiritual, reaching its fullness in a close and everlasting embrace. It involves both the soul and the body, entailing thirst and hunger. Beginning with a cry to God and the confession "You are my God," the poet expresses a deep and personal yearning for God's presence (verse 1). "My soul thirsts for you, my flesh faints for you." The need for God is as instinctual and relentless as if one were searching for water in a dry, sun-baked wilderness. Just as water is fertility in parched ground, without the presence of God the soul cannot live.

The poet knows that he experiences God's presence in the sanctuary (verse 2). There he encounters the divine power and glory. The psalmist declares to God, "Your steadfast love is better than life" (verse 3). Although life is often understood as the summary of all God's gifts, here the experience of God's love transcends even life itself. So, the poet vows to always seek and stay close to God through liturgical actions like vocal praise, blessings, lifted hands, and invocation of God's name (verse 4).

After describing the longing for God as a deep thirst, the poet turns to hunger, speaking of worshiping God as "a rich feast" (verse 5). The psalmist is referring to the communion sacrifices of the temple in which those offering the sacrifice eat the flesh of the sacrifice in a sacred meal. The poet continues to deepen his expression of intimacy with God as he speaks about his thoughts of God persisting through the night, keeping him wakeful even as the sentinels of Jerusalem announce the successive watches as night progresses (verse 6). The psalmist continues to express his desire for closeness with God as he joyfully sings in the shadow of God's protective wings (verse 7). And, in an exquisitely tender image, the soul "clings" to God, whose right hand steadies him (verse 8).

Following the poet's sublime expressions of personal longing for God and of deep union with God, he introduces his enemies, from whom he seeks God's protective presence (verses 9–11). He is confident that the adversaries will be defeated, while the king and all who serve him will rejoice and exult in God. Mouths that speak falsehood will be stopped up, while mouths that give praise to God are opened.

These final verses remind us that our relationship with God is not just a personal, interior experience but rather involves our outer lives in communion with others. While we seek an ever more intense and close relationship with God, both enemies and allies surround us. The life of faith engages a vertical longing for God and a horizontal association with friends and foes.

Reflection and discussion

- In what ways do the sensations of thirst and hunger express my desire for the presence of God?

- When have I experienced such an intimate unity with God?

- How do the psalmist's words "Your steadfast love is better than life" express the heart of the martyrs?

Prayer

O God, my God, I lift up my hands and call on your name. Implant within me a deep desire for your presence and help me to thirst for you like a dry, parched land yearns for life-giving water.

SUGGESTIONS FOR FACILITATORS, GROUP SESSION 3

1. Welcome group members and ask if anyone has any announcements to make.

2. You may want to pray this prayer as a group:
O God our help in ages past, may the memory of your steadfast love and faithfulness sustain our confidence and hope for the future. Protect your people from the snares of evil, cleanse us from sin, create a clean heart within us, and shelter us in the shadow of your wings. As we lift our hands and hearts to call upon your name, implant within us a deep desire to live in you and give you praise. May your glory be exalted above the heavens and over all the earth as you guide your people to the place of your eternal dwelling.

3. Ask one or both of the following questions:
    - Which thought from the lessons this week stands out most memorably to you?
    - What is the most important lesson you learned through your study this week?

4. Discuss lessons 7 through 12. Choose one or more of the questions for reflection and discussion from each lesson to discuss as a group. You may want to ask group members which question was most challenging or helpful to them as you review each lesson.

5. Remember that there are no definitive answers for these discussion questions. The insights of group members will add to the understanding of all. None of these questions requires an expert.

6. After talking about each lesson, instruct group members to complete lessons 13 through 18 on their own during the six days before the next group meeting. They should write out their own answers to the questions as preparation for next week's group discussion.

7. Ask the group if anyone is having any particular problems with the Bible study during the week. You may want to share advice and encouragement within the group.

8. Conclude by praying aloud together the prayer at the end of one of the lessons discussed. You may add to the prayer based on the sharing that has occurred in the group.

Those who live at earth's farthest bounds are awed by your signs;
you make the gateways of the morning and the evening shout for joy.

PSALM 65:8

Giving Thanks to the Lord of All the Earth

PSALM 65

1 *Praise is due to you,*
O God, in Zion;
and to you shall vows be performed,
2 *O you who answer prayer!*
To you all flesh shall come.
3 *When deeds of iniquity overwhelm us,*
you forgive our transgressions.
4 *Happy are those whom you choose and bring near*
to live in your courts.
We shall be satisfied with the goodness of your house,
your holy temple.

5 *By awesome deeds you answer us with deliverance,*
O God of our salvation;
you are the hope of all the ends of the earth
and of the farthest seas.
6 *By your strength you established the mountains;*
you are girded with might.
7 *You silence the roaring of the seas,*
the roaring of their waves,
the tumult of the peoples.

8 Those who live at earth's farthest bounds are awed by your signs;
you make the gateways of the morning and the evening shout for joy.

9 You visit the earth and water it,
you greatly enrich it;
the river of God is full of water;
you provide the people with grain,
for so you have prepared it.
10 You water its furrows abundantly,
settling its ridges,
softening it with showers,
and blessing its growth.
11 You crown the year with your bounty;
your wagon tracks overflow with richness.
12 The pastures of the wilderness overflow,
the hills gird themselves with joy,
13 the meadows clothe themselves with flocks,
the valleys deck themselves with grain,
they shout and sing together for joy.

The hymn is addressed to God and consists of three movements. In the first, the congregation celebrates God's goodness in the temple (verses 1–4). In the second, they honor God's creative power throughout the earth (verses 5–8). And in the third, God's people express gratitude for God's bountiful gifts of rain and harvest (verses 9–12). Each movement concludes with a description of the effects of God's activity—for the worshiping crowds at the temple (verse 4), for people throughout the world (verse 8), and for fertile land (verses 12–13). The occasion of the hymn is offering thanks to God for the spring or autumn harvest.

The initial focus is on Zion, the presence of God manifested at the temple in Jerusalem. The people have ascended from their homes and farms to offer due praise to God. As their grateful response to God for answering their prayers, they perform their vows, the thanksgiving offering of the first fruits of their fields and flocks (verses 1–2). Whenever worshipers come to God, they come burdened with their sins. Yet, standing in God's presence, they confidently request and receive God's forgiveness for their iniquity (verse 3). Finally, they are blessed with joy because they have been chosen to dwell in the courts of their divine King. Addressing God, they express their happiness to settle in "your courts," "your house," and "your holy temple" (verse 4). Those who offer their gifts at the temple share them in a communion sacrifice, ending in a sacred meal shared with God. The worshipers are satisfied with the goodness of this divine domestic setting in the courts of the temple.

The focus of the hymn then widens from the temple to the farthest reach of the earth and seas (verse 5). God's creative power is described as that of a divine warrior, delivering his people from the chaos of destruction with awesome deeds. Indeed, the Bible contains more creation accounts than just those in the opening chapters of Genesis. With divine strength, God established the mountains as pillars that stabilize the earth above the threatening waters (verse 6). He silences "the roaring of the seas" and establishes order among "the tumult of the peoples," holding everything in check (verse 7). In this dynamic view of creation, its order and stability cannot be taken for granted. The threat of chaos continually requires God to exert his strength. The "God of our salvation" persistently keeps the cosmos in order to protect his people. As a result of God's mighty "signs," those who live at the farthest bounds of East and West are amazed (verse 8). Even the dawn and sunset, "the gateways of the morning and the evening," shout with joy at the wondrous works of God.

The final movement of the hymn moves from the farthest reaches of the world to the harvested fields of God's people (verse 9). How wonderful that the architect of the cosmos stoops to water the land and inspect the harvest! There is a correlation between the roaring seas and rain for the crops, between the distant mountains and the fertilized fields, between the tumult of the peoples and the praise of God's people offering the first fruits of the harvest. The chaotic waters are channeled into "the river of God" and into gentle life-giving rains. God visits the earth, waters it, enriches it, and provides its people with grain. By watering its "furrows abundantly, settling its ridges, softening it with showers, and blessing its growth," God, the divine farmer, brings in the sheaves for his people (verse 10). As the farm wagon carries its bounty, it leaves heavy tracks as a sign of its load of blessings (verse 11). The earth dresses itself in festive attire for the harvest feast: the hills joyfully "gird themselves," the meadows "clothe themselves" with flocks of sheep, and the valleys "deck themselves" with grain (verses 12–13).

The psalm reminds us moderns not to view the world as a commodity to be used at our convenience. The earth is a gift from God, the divine warrior and farmer, made fertile and fruitful by him. In this vision of creation, even the dawn and sunset "shout for joy," and the pastures, hills, meadows, and valleys "shout and sing together for joy." All the earth gives grateful praise as God's people present their thanksgiving offerings in the temple courts and sing this psalm.

Reflection and discussion

- What is the relationship between the people's offerings in the temple and the created fruitfulness of all the earth?

- How does God show himself as both a divine warrior and a divine farmer today?

- What can I offer to God to express my gratitude for his bountiful gifts?

Prayer

O God of the mountains and valleys, of the fields and the flocks, I sing and shout your praises with gratitude in my heart. Give success to the work of my hands and receive my thanksgiving offering in the courts of your heavenly temple.

I will call to mind the deeds of the Lord; I will remember your wonders of old. I will meditate on all your work, and muse on your mighty deeds. PSALM 77:11–12

Turning to God in Despair and in Hope

PSALM 77

1 *I cry aloud to God,*
aloud to God, that he may hear me.
2 *In the day of my trouble I seek the Lord;*
in the night my hand is stretched out without wearying;
my soul refuses to be comforted.
3 *I think of God, and I moan;*
I meditate, and my spirit faints. Selah

4 *You keep my eyelids from closing;*
I am so troubled that I cannot speak.
5 *I consider the days of old,*
and remember the years of long ago.
6 *I commune with my heart in the night;*
I meditate and search my spirit:
7 *"Will the Lord spurn forever,*
and never again be favorable?
8 *Has his steadfast love ceased forever?*
Are his promises at an end for all time?
9 *Has God forgotten to be gracious?*
Has he in anger shut up his compassion?" Selah

10 *And I say, "It is my grief*
that the right hand of the Most High has changed."

11 *I will call to mind the deeds of the Lord;*
I will remember your wonders of old.
12 *I will meditate on all your work,*
and muse on your mighty deeds.
13 *Your way, O God, is holy.*
What god is so great as our God?
14 *You are the God who works wonders;*
you have displayed your might among the peoples.
15 *With your strong arm you redeemed your people,*
the descendants of Jacob and Joseph. Selah

16 *When the waters saw you, O God,*
when the waters saw you, they were afraid;
the very deep trembled.
17 *The clouds poured out water;*
the skies thundered;
your arrows flashed on every side.
18 *The crash of your thunder was in the whirlwind;*
your lightnings lit up the world;
the earth trembled and shook.
19 *Your way was through the sea,*
your path, through the mighty waters;
yet your footprints were unseen.
20 *You led your people like a flock*
by the hand of Moses and Aaron.

The psalm opens with a loud cry, seeking to be heard by God. We can feel the anguish of the psalmist's distress (verses 1–4). These gloomy musings yield only an aching longing, leaving the poet restless, speechless, and lost in nostalgia. The troubled sleeper stretches out his hand toward God in the night, pleading for God's response. Tossing and turning, his troubled soul moans, fretting over God's seeming absence and silence.

The unsatisfied prayer of the psalmist brings no comfort, so he turns to the past and searches there for an answer (verses 5–6). He pours out his anxious questions: Will the Lord reject me forever? Has the steadfast love of God now ceased? The questions express the most frightful fears that can come upon the soul: Has God abandoned me (verses 7–9)? The psalmist seems on the edge of despair. The questions evoke the list of attributes that have characterized the Lord's dealings with Israel through the ages: divine favor, steadfast love, covenant promises, graciousness, and compassion. The questions reach their climax in a distressing conclusion: "It is my grief that the right hand of the Most High has changed" (verse 10). God's "right hand" is the divine power by which he has always brought protection and deliverance to his people. If God's ways have changed, the psalmist wonders if God has changed his mind about his people.

In an attempt to deal with his distress, the poet resolves to evoke in his mind the history of God's ways with Israel in the past (verse 11–12). In this deep sense of what it means to "remember," the deeds of God in the past are drawn into the present with all their power and grace. As he re-presents God's saving actions by chanting the words of the psalm, the poet is able to cope with his awful questions and begin to trust again. By calling to mind God's deeds, remembering, meditating, and musing in melodic prayer addressed to God, the psalmist experiences God's saving power in his own life.

God's way is "holy," transcending human ways (verse 13). The primal saving event that brought Israel into existence as a people was the wonders God worked through the mighty waters at the sea (verses 14–20). Professing faith in God's redeeming events in the past leads to confident faith in what God is always doing in the present. The circumstances of the psalmist that seemed without a way out are now guided by faith and open to hope.

This recollection of God's actions for his people illumines the dark night of the psalmist just as the pillar of fire accompanied God's people through the desert. Yet, as the poet says to God, "Your footprints were unseen" (verse 19). As God mysteriously guided the people in the way of the wilderness, God continues to open a route through raging waters. The poet and all the readers of his psalm must now follow God through the storm, whirlwind, lightning, and thunder, where only God knows the way. In the end, the poet's problem is not solved; rather, it is dissolved in the light of a more intense and profound encounter with God.

Reflection and discussion

- Which of the psalmist's questions (verses 7–9) have kept me awake at night?

- Why did the psalmist turn to the redeeming events of Israel at the sea to relieve his own distress?

- How can praying psalms or other biblical passages relieve my anguished spirit?

Prayer

I cry out to you, O God, in times of trouble. You are the God who works wonders, and you display your might among the peoples. By meditation on your deeds in Scripture, help me to trust in your saving presence.

Turn again, O God of hosts; look down from heaven, and see; have regard for this vine, the stock that your right hand planted.
PSALM 80:14–15

Plea to Restore God's Vineyard

PSALM 80

1 *Give ear, O Shepherd of Israel,*
you who lead Joseph like a flock!
You who are enthroned upon the cherubim, shine forth
2 *before Ephraim and Benjamin and Manasseh.*
Stir up your might,
and come to save us!

3 *Restore us, O God;*
let your face shine, that we may be saved.

4 *O Lord God of hosts,*
how long will you be angry with your people's prayers?
5 *You have fed them with the bread of tears,*
and given them tears to drink in full measure.
6 *You make us the scorn of our neighbors;*
our enemies laugh among themselves.

7 *Restore us, O God of hosts;*
let your face shine, that we may be saved.

8 *You brought a vine out of Egypt;*
you drove out the nations and planted it.

9You cleared the ground for it;
it took deep root and filled the land.
10The mountains were covered with its shade,
the mighty cedars with its branches;
11it sent out its branches to the sea,
and its shoots to the River.
12Why then have you broken down its walls,
so that all who pass along the way pluck its fruit?
13The boar from the forest ravages it,
and all that move in the field feed on it.

14Turn again, O God of hosts;
look down from heaven, and see;
have regard for this vine,
15the stock that your right hand planted.
16They have burned it with fire, they have cut it down;
may they perish at the rebuke of your countenance.
17But let your hand be upon the one at your right hand,
the one whom you made strong for yourself.
18Then we will never turn back from you;
give us life, and we will call on your name.

19Restore us, O Lord God of hosts;
let your face shine, that we may be saved.

The psalm offers a prayer for the restoration of God's people from a national disaster. Its message is encapsulated in the repeating refrain "Restore us, O God; let your face shine, that we may be saved," with the address to God slightly expanded with each repetition (verses 3, 7, 19). The prayer expresses the longing to return to the previous relationship between God and his covenanted people. The choral plea expresses faith that only God's personal care and protection can save his people from destruction. Since the psalm doesn't identify any particular tragedy, the psalm can be prayed in any situation of trouble. "Restore us, O God" can range in meaning from the physical rebuilding after exile to spiritual renewal.

God is first addressed as Israel's Shepherd, the one invisibly enthroned above the ark of the covenant in the presence of the tribes of Israel (verses 1–2). Four imperatives addressed to God enforce the sense of urgency: "Give ear," "shine forth," "stir up your might," and "restore us." God needs to pay attention and do something. The poet then asks the question, typical of so many prayers of complaint, "How long?" (verse 4). How long will God vent his anger while the people suffer? Their food and drink is a diet of "bread of tears" and "tears to drink," humiliation from neighbors and ridicule from enemies (verses 5–6).

The imagery of God then shifts to that of a winegrower, caring for the vine of Israel, uprooting his people from Egypt and transplanting them in their own land (verse 8). The imagery of Israel as a vine is well attested throughout the writings of Israel's prophets. The divine vinedresser took such care of the grapevine that it took deep root and filled the land (verse 9). The thriving branches of the vine covered the mountains and cedars of the land, from the Mediterranean Sea to the Jordan River (verses 10–11). Yet now, the walls that protected the vine are now broken down, and all who pass by take its treasure as spoils (verse 12). Israel's enemies ravage the vine, like a wild boar feeding on its fruits (verse 13).

The psalmist calls upon God, who appears to be absent, to "turn again" and "have regard for this vine" that he planted (verses 14–15). If Israel is to survive this disaster, it will be through God's power and not its own. Although the nation has been cut down and burned with fire, they call upon God to strengthen or restore the king, "the one at your right hand, the one whom you made strong for yourself" (verses 16–17). Later Jewish tradition interpreted this text as an expression of hope for the Messiah, the future royal king, who would save them from their enemies and restore them to peace.

The lament concludes with the people's promise of faithfulness and praise if they are restored to life (verse 18). The prayer calls on God to repent, to turn again to his former ways with Israel and take responsibility for the vine he planted.

Reflection and discussion

- When has God felt absent, asleep, detached, or indifferent to me?

- What aspects of the grapevine make it such an apt symbol for the people of God?

- What characteristics of this psalm enable it to be used to lament the afflicted people of God at any time of trouble throughout history?

Prayer

O Lord God of the heavenly hosts, come and save your people in distress. You are the vine-grower, and Christ united with his church is your vine. Help me abide in your Son and bear much fruit for the vine.

I am the Lord your God, who brought you up out of the land of Egypt. Open your mouth wide and I will fill it. PSALM 81:10

Hear, O My People, and Listen to Me

PSALM 81

1 *Sing aloud to God our strength;*
shout for joy to the God of Jacob.
2 *Raise a song, sound the tambourine,*
the sweet lyre with the harp.
3 *Blow the trumpet at the new moon,*
at the full moon, on our festal day.
4 *For it is a statute for Israel,*
an ordinance of the God of Jacob.
5 *He made it a decree in Joseph,*
when he went out over the land of Egypt.

I hear a voice I had not known:
6 *"I relieved your shoulder of the burden;*
your hands were freed from the basket.
7 *In distress you called, and I rescued you;*
I answered you in the secret place of thunder;
I tested you at the waters of Meribah. Selah
8 *Hear, O my people, while I admonish you;*
O Israel, if you would but listen to me!
9 *There shall be no strange god among you;*
you shall not bow down to a foreign god.

10*I am the Lord your God,*
who brought you up out of the land of Egypt.
Open your mouth wide and I will fill it.

11*"But my people did not listen to my voice;*
Israel would not submit to me.
12*So I gave them over to their stubborn hearts,*
to follow their own counsels.
13*O that my people would listen to me,*
that Israel would walk in my ways!
14*Then I would quickly subdue their enemies,*
and turn my hand against their foes.
15*Those who hate the Lord would cringe before him,*
and their doom would last forever.
16*I would feed you with the finest of the wheat,*
and with honey from the rock I would satisfy you."

The opening call to worship makes clear that the setting is the festival liturgy of God's people. First, the assembly is called to "sing aloud," "shout for joy," and "raise a song" in full-throated praise of God (verses 1–2). Second, they are to play instruments to accompany the song: tambourine, lyre, harp, and trumpet (verses 2–3). Third, the occasion of their worship is "the new moon," "the full moon," "our festal day." And fourth, the reasons for worship are "a statute," "an ordinance," and "a decree" that God has given to his people (verses 4–5). The implication is that worship is essential for Israel's covenant obedience to God.

The leader of worship then introduces the speaker for the assembly: "I hear a voice I had not known." Hereafter, the voice throughout the psalm is that of God. The divine speaker then recounts what he has done for Israel. "I relieved" them from their oppressive labor, the baskets of clay bricks they had to carry (verse 6). "I rescued" them when my people called on me in their distress (verse 7). "I answered" them, giving them the Torah at Mount Sinai. "I tested" them when they doubted whether I could quench their thirst in the wilderness.

In light of all that God has done for his people, God calls them to "hear" and to "listen," words that will be repeated throughout the address (verse 8). If one truly hears God's word, then one follows God's word. The failure to truly listen leads to disobedience. So, the prophets of Israel repeatedly pronounce judgment upon those who "have ears but do not hear." God admonishes his people by repeating the demands of the first commandment. They must not receive strange gods among them or bow down in worship to any god but the Lord. When they worship only the God who rescued them from the slavery of Egypt, their needs will be satisfied (verses 9–10).

Tragically, God's people did not "listen" to God's word, and so they did not obey God (verse 11). Since Israel did not follow God's counsel, God permits them "to follow their own counsels," with undeniably devastating results (verse 12). By forfeiting their covenant loyalty to God, they forfeit God's covenant promises. God laments, "O that my people would listen to me, that Israel would walk in my ways!" (verse 13). How different things would be! Instead of distress, Israel would find its enemies subdued and its agriculture bountiful (verses 14–16).

The psalm reminds us that we are Israel; we are the people of God addressed in the psalm. We might not have actual physical enemies and foes, but there are always enemies within us. If we would truly hear God's word and follow it, how quickly God would defeat those ancient foes, and we would feed on the finest wheat and enjoy the sweet honey of God's plenty. The psalm remains open-ended. Although Israel forfeited their opportunity with God, the congregation hearing this psalm in every age can still make the right choice. The festival assembly is the time for the congregation to decide anew whether they will follow the way of their past refusal to hear God's word or listen to God and dedicate themselves to following his ways.

Reflection and discussion

- What impact would this psalm make when performed at the temple in Jerusalem at Israel's annual festivals?

- What happens when God's people do not "hear" God's word?

- What indicates that this psalm is open-ended and incomplete? Why does the psalm remain incomplete?

Prayer

Lord God of Israel, you speak your word, but so often I fail to listen to your voice. Open my ears to truly hear your voice and worship you alone. May I renew your covenant and receive your generous blessings.

Steadfast love and faithfulness will meet; righteousness and peace will kiss each other. Faithfulness will spring up from the ground, and righteousness will look down from the sky. PSALM 85:10–11

Pilgrims Yearn for the Dwelling Place of God

PSALM 84

1*How lovely is your dwelling place,*
O Lord of hosts!
2*My soul longs, indeed it faints*
for the courts of the Lord;
my heart and my flesh sing for joy
to the living God.

3*Even the sparrow finds a home,*
and the swallow a nest for herself,
where she may lay her young,
at your altars, O Lord of hosts,
my King and my God.
4*Happy are those who live in your house,*
ever singing your praise. Selah

5*Happy are those whose strength is in you,*
in whose heart are the highways to Zion.
6*As they go through the valley of Baca*
they make it a place of springs;
the early rain also covers it with pools.
7*They go from strength to strength;*
the God of gods will be seen in Zion.

8 *O Lord God of hosts, hear my prayer;*
give ear, O God of Jacob! Selah
9 *Behold our shield, O God;*
look on the face of your anointed.

10 *For a day in your courts is better*
than a thousand elsewhere.
I would rather be a doorkeeper in the house of my God
than live in the tents of wickedness.
11 *For the Lord God is a sun and shield;*
he bestows favor and honor.
No good thing does the Lord withhold
from those who walk uprightly.
12 *O Lord of hosts,*
happy is everyone who trusts in you.

PSALM 85

1 *Lord, you were favorable to your land;*
you restored the fortunes of Jacob.
2 *You forgave the iniquity of your people;*
you pardoned all their sin. Selah
3 *You withdrew all your wrath;*
you turned from your hot anger.

4 *Restore us again, O God of our salvation,*
and put away your indignation toward us.
5 *Will you be angry with us forever?*
Will you prolong your anger to all generations?
6 *Will you not revive us again,*
so that your people may rejoice in you?
7 *Show us your steadfast love, O Lord,*
and grant us your salvation.

8 *Let me hear what God the Lord will speak,*
for he will speak peace to his people, to his faithful,
to those who turn to him in their hearts.

[9]*Surely his salvation is at hand for those who fear him,*
that his glory may dwell in our land.

[10]*Steadfast love and faithfulness will meet;*
righteousness and peace will kiss each other.
[11]*Faithfulness will spring up from the ground,*
and righteousness will look down from the sky.
[12]*The Lord will give what is good,*
and our land will yield its increase.
[13]*Righteousness will go before him,*
and will make a path for his steps.

Psalm 84 was sung by pilgrims traveling up to Jerusalem, to the "dwelling place" of the Lord of hosts (84:1). This belief in the divine presence of God in the temple prompted a deep desire to travel there on pilgrimage for Israel's feasts (84:2). The psalmist's yearning encompasses soul, heart, and flesh, alternately fainting and singing for joy. Even delicate sparrows and swallows seek the temple courts to build their nests, finding protection and blessing near God's altars for their young (84:3). In the first of three beatitudes, the psalmist acclaims, "Happy are those" who live at God's dwelling place, both chanting pilgrims and chirping birds, together singing God's praises (84:4).

The second stanza opens with another beatitude: "Happy are those" who find in God their strength for the journey. God's presence beckons them onward as they long to travel the highways that lead to Jerusalem (84:5). The joy of the pilgrims brings life to the dry valley, filling it with springs and vital rain (84:6). As they approach the city, their anticipation gathers, and "they go from strength to strength" (84:7).

The pilgrims' longing finds fulfillment at the temple, as they pray and extol the Lord God of hosts (84:8). The king, appointed by God to care for the nation, is in attendance. He is the "shield" of the people, protecting and defending them, and the "anointed" of God, chosen to carry out the divine will for Israel (84:9).

The concluding verses proclaim the immeasurable value of spending even the briefest moments in God's presence (84:10). One day with God is better than a thousand days away from him. Even standing at the edge of God's house as a doorkeeper is better than living comfortably in the houses of the wicked. Naming God as the "Lord of hosts" evokes images of God as the commander of the armies of heaven and as the divine king invisibly enthroned in the temple above the ark of the covenant. He is acclaimed as "sun and shield," expressing his dominion in the heavens and his protection over the earth (84:11). Those who walk uprightly with integrity may now enter the temple and receive God's blessings. The prayer concludes with another comforting beatitude: "Happy is everyone who trusts in you" (84:12).

Psalm 85 expresses the tension of living between promise and fulfillment. God has already given salvation to his people, yet we are in daily need of God's saving presence. The psalm begins by expressing gratitude to God for all the past favors granted to his people (85:1–3). So often he forgave his people, withdrawing his just anger and pardoning them with mercy. Even when they were in exile, God forgave their iniquity and restored their fortunes in their own land.

But now, they are yet again in need of God's saving help (85:4–7). "Restore us again," they cry, "O God of our salvation." Once more they implore God to withdraw his "anger" and renew his "steadfast love." Even though God restored his people after their exile, they are forever in need of God's merciful pardon. "Revive us again," they cry, pleading with God to enable them to rejoice in his salvation.

While the first half of the psalm consists of prayer addressed to God, the second half anticipates God's response (85:8–13). The psalmist expresses confidence that God will answer the prayers of those who faithfully turn to him: "Surely his salvation is at hand for those who fear him, that his glory may dwell in our land." They remain faithful to God in spite of experiences that seem to contradict God's promises of covenant blessings. In beautiful poetry, the divine attributes of steadfast love, faithfulness, righteousness, and peace are personified and joyfully greet each other. When God sends his steadfast love to the earth, faithfulness springs up from the ground. As righteousness looks down from the sky, the earth responds with peace. For God's worshipers, the heavens and the earth are not separate because God is the Lord of all. Both the blessings of God and human response are necessary for the land to yield its increase and for the natural world to flourish.

Reflection and discussion

- Why is pilgrimage a richer experience than ordinary travel? Why does God invite his people to go on pilgrimage?

- God's wrath in the psalms is always a righteous anger in the face of evil. How can I develop an appropriate respect for God's just anger?

- If salvation is the dynamic activity of steadfast love, faithfulness, righteousness, and peace given to us by God, why are we still always in need of salvation?

Prayer

Restore us again, O God of our salvation, and put away your righteous anger toward us. Show us your steadfast love, faithfulness, righteousness, and peace so that we may experience your salvation and rejoice in you.

**Give ear, O Lord, to my prayer; listen to my cry of supplication.
In the day of my trouble I call on you, for you will answer me.**
PSALM 86:6–7

All Nations Shall Come and Adore the Lord

PSALM 86

1 *Incline your ear, O Lord, and answer me,*
for I am poor and needy.
2 *Preserve my life, for I am devoted to you;*
save your servant who trusts in you.
You are my God; 3 *be gracious to me, O Lord,*
for to you do I cry all day long.
4 *Gladden the soul of your servant,*
for to you, O Lord, I lift up my soul.
5 *For you, O Lord, are good and forgiving,*
abounding in steadfast love to all who call on you.
6 *Give ear, O Lord, to my prayer;*
listen to my cry of supplication.
7 *In the day of my trouble I call on you,*
for you will answer me.

8 *There is none like you among the gods, O Lord,*
nor are there any works like yours.
9 *All the nations you have made shall come*
and bow down before you, O Lord,
and shall glorify your name.

10 *For you are great and do wondrous things;*
you alone are God.
11 *Teach me your way, O Lord,*
that I may walk in your truth;
give me an undivided heart to revere your name.
12 *I give thanks to you, O Lord my God, with my whole heart,*
and I will glorify your name forever.
13 *For great is your steadfast love toward me;*
you have delivered my soul from the depths of Sheol.

14 *O God, the insolent rise up against me;*
a band of ruffians seeks my life,
and they do not set you before them.
15 *But you, O Lord, are a God merciful and gracious,*
slow to anger and abounding in steadfast love and faithfulness.
16 *Turn to me and be gracious to me;*
give your strength to your servant;
save the child of your serving girl.
17 *Show me a sign of your favor,*
so that those who hate me may see it and be put to shame,
because you, Lord, have helped me and comforted me.

PSALM 87

1 *On the holy mount stands the city he founded;*
2 *the Lord loves the gates of Zion*
more than all the dwellings of Jacob.
3 *Glorious things are spoken of you,*
O city of God. Selah

4 *Among those who know me I mention Rahab and Babylon;*
Philistia too, and Tyre, with Ethiopia—
"This one was born there," they say.

5 *And of Zion it shall be said,*
"This one and that one were born in it";
for the Most High himself will establish it.

6 The Lord records, as he registers the peoples,
"This one was born there." Selah

7 Singers and dancers alike say,
"All my springs are in you."

Psalm 86 is a prayer of lament, consisting of heartfelt pleas in a time of need and interspersed with traditional expressions of God's saving goodness. In this form, it shows the value of spontaneous prayer to God mixed with more customary prayers of praise and trust. It serves as a model prayer for anyone living within the covenant between God and his people. As a morning prayer, it forms our hearts for a day that might bring with it misunderstandings, fatigue, and problems.

The opening section is marked by a series of petitions: "incline your ear" and "answer me," "preserve my life," "save your servant," "be gracious to me," "lift up my soul," "give ear to my prayer," and "listen to my cry" (86:1–4, 6). Each plea is supported by a statement about the one who prays in relationship to God: "for I am poor and needy," "for I am devoted to you," "for to you I cry," for to you "I lift up my soul." The one who prays disavows all self-sufficiency and admits that life is totally dependent on God. Inserted within these petitions are traditional phrases describing God as "good and forgiving, abounding in steadfast love to all who call on [God]," describing a dependable God of unchanging character through generations of believers (86:5). Each petition is prayed in confidence that God will respond: "I call on you, for you will answer me" (86:7).

The center of the psalm is a prayer of pure praise, expanding the characteristics of God (86:8–10). The personal God who hears and answers the prayers of his people is also the universal and only God. God alone works with unlimited power and unrivaled authority. The Lord is the creator of all the nations, and all peoples will, in due time, offer him homage and glorify his name.

The final section returns to petitions, pleading not only for deliverance in time of trouble, but also for a lifestyle and inner character that will enable the one praying to offer God praise and thanks. The psalmist prays to God, "Teach me your way" and "give me an undivided heart" (86:11). Such understanding of God's ways and purity of heart enables the one praying to give wholehearted thanks to God and to glorify God's name forever (86:12). The psalmist seeks a single heart to worship the one God.

Again, inserted within these petitions are the traditional phrases describing God's character through all generations: "merciful and gracious, slow to anger and abounding in steadfast love and faithfulness" (86:15). Because of this universal and, at the same time, personal divine love, every person who prays this psalm can petition God in the same way as the psalmist: "Turn to me and be gracious to me; give your strength to your servant; save the child of your serving girl" (86:16). In every generation, God's people may cry out to him, "Show me a sign of your favor...because you, Lord, have helped and comforted me" (86:17).

Psalm 87 is a song written for a liturgical celebration in Jerusalem. A procession of pilgrims, accompanied by "singers and dancers," rejoices in Zion as the source of their joy and blessings. Because Jerusalem was founded by God "on the holy mount," it is proclaimed as the "city of God" (87:1–3). God's choice of Zion and God's preference for her over all the other shrines of the land is marvelously beyond explanation.

The second half of the psalm proclaims Jerusalem as the spiritual home for people who live in all the nations throughout the world (87:4–7). God is envisioned registering the people of the various nations, declaring that they were born in Jerusalem. This theological metaphor asserts that those who acknowledge the Lord have birthright status in Zion, no matter where they live. God's declaration that "this one was born there" is repeated three times as God records their status.

Shockingly, the roll call of those who are spiritually reborn in Jerusalem begins with Israel's archenemies. Egypt (called Rahab) and Babylonia, the oppressors of Israel during the exodus and the exile, now "know" God and are declared naturalized citizens of God's city. The same is said for warring Philistia, proud and wealthy Tyre, and distant Ethiopia. The hopes envisioned by the previous psalm are being fulfilled: "All the nations you have made shall come and bow down before you, O Lord, and shall glorify your name" (86:9). The foreign nations join the procession of the citizens in Zion. Jerusalem's destiny is an image of a remodeled world in which all the nations are converted into members of the one family of God.

Reflection and discussion

- Try praying Psalm 86 through the mind and heart of Jesus, the Suffering Servant of Israel. What difference does this experience make?

- Why does the psalmist pray for "an undivided heart" (86:11)? In what ways does my heart seem divided or even broken? What could restore the unity of my heart so that I may give thanks to God "with my whole heart" (86:12)?

- In what ways does Psalm 87 encourage me to become more inclusive of people who are different from me?

Prayer

O Lord, you are merciful and gracious, slow to anger and abounding in steadfast love and faithfulness. Teach me your ways, that I may walk in your truth. Give me an undivided heart to revere your name.

SUGGESTIONS FOR FACILITATORS, GROUP SESSION 4

1. Welcome group members and ask if anyone has any questions, announcements, or requests.

2. You may want to pray this prayer as a group:
   Merciful and gracious Lord, you speak your word to your people, but so often we fail to listen to your voice. By meditating on your words and deeds in Scripture, show us your steadfast love, faithfulness, righteousness, salvation, and peace. Open our ears to truly hear your voice and worship you alone. May we walk in your truth, and may we sing and shout your praises with gratitude in our hearts. Give success to the work of our hands, and receive our thanksgiving offering in the courts of your heavenly temple.

3. Ask one or both of the following questions:
   - What is the most difficult part of this study for you?
   - What insights stand out for you from the lessons this week?

4. Discuss lessons 13 through 18. Choose one or more of the questions for reflection and discussion from each lesson to discuss as a group. You may want to ask group members which question was most challenging or helpful for them as you review each lesson.

5. Keep the discussion moving but allow time for the questions that provoke the most discussion. Encourage the group members to use "I" language in their responses.

6. After talking over each lesson, instruct group members to complete lessons 19 through 24 on their own during the six days before the next group meeting. They should write out their own answers to the questions as preparation for next week's session.

7. Ask the group what encouragement they need for the coming week. Ask the members to pray for the needs of one another during the week.

8. Conclude by praying aloud together the prayer at the end of one of the lessons discussed. You may choose to conclude the prayer by asking members to pray aloud any requests they may have.

Turn, O Lord! How long? Have compassion on your servants! Satisfy us in the morning with your steadfast love, so that we may rejoice and be glad all our days. PSALM 90:13–14

A Thousand Years Like a Watch in the Night

PSALM 90

1*Lord, you have been our dwelling place*
in all generations.
2*Before the mountains were brought forth,*
or ever you had formed the earth and the world,
from everlasting to everlasting you are God.

3*You turn us back to dust,*
and say, "Turn back, you mortals."
4*For a thousand years in your sight*
are like yesterday when it is past,
or like a watch in the night.

5*You sweep them away; they are like a dream,*
like grass that is renewed in the morning;
6*in the morning it flourishes and is renewed;*
in the evening it fades and withers.

7*For we are consumed by your anger;*
by your wrath we are overwhelmed.
8*You have set our iniquities before you,*
our secret sins in the light of your countenance.

9 For all our days pass away under your wrath;
our years come to an end like a sigh.
10 The days of our life are seventy years,
or perhaps eighty, if we are strong;
even then their span is only toil and trouble;
they are soon gone, and we fly away.

11 Who considers the power of your anger?
Your wrath is as great as the fear that is due you.
12 So teach us to count our days
that we may gain a wise heart.

13 Turn, O Lord! How long?
Have compassion on your servants!
14 Satisfy us in the morning with your steadfast love,
so that we may rejoice and be glad all our days.
15 Make us glad as many days as you have afflicted us,
and as many years as we have seen evil.
16 Let your work be manifest to your servants,
and your glorious power to their children.
17 Let the favor of the Lord our God be upon us,
and prosper for us the work of our hands—
O prosper the work of our hands!

The heart of this prayer is the brevity and frailty of life, one of the topics most expressed by poetry, most explored by philosophy, and most felt by human experience in every age. It is enough to think of some extraordinary passages from the book of Job: "For inquire now of bygone generations, and consider what their ancestors have found; for we are but of yesterday, and we know nothing, for our days on earth are but a shadow" (Job 8:8–9). Yet, this prayer probes the transience of human life from the perspective of one who lives in the shadow of the eternal God. From this viewpoint of eternity, deep wisdom can be derived from this contemplation of time.

The opening verses contrast the permanence of God with the transitory time of humanity. In every generation, God has been the "dwelling place" of his people, the one who preserves and protects them (verses 1–2). As creator of the world, God precedes all that exists. God was present when the ancient mountains emerged and when the earth was brought forth. In contrast to God's eternity, human life is fleeting. As a consequence of sin, humans return to the dust from which they were taken. As Genesis states, "You are dust, and to dust you shall return" (Genesis 3:19). The creator who shapes the human creature with splendor and complexity is also the God who turns them back to the dust of death (verse 3). The poet emphasizes the brief human lifespan by referring to the standard measures of time. What to humans is a thousand years to God is like a day or like a watch in the night (verse 4). Life passes as quickly as a fleeting dream or like the grass that springs afresh in the morning, but by evening it is cut down by the sickle and reduced to a heap of hay (verses 5–6).

This human frailty, as the Scriptures often teach, is associated with the sin of humanity. For this reason, God's righteous anger and judgment seem to overshadow our lives (verses 7–9). Our days, months, and years pass quickly, and death comes "like a sigh." The average lifespan in the ancient world was generally less than fifty years. So, by citing the measure of life as seventy or eighty years, the psalmist implies that even relatively long lives are brief in comparison to eternity (verse 10). Even a long span of life is merely an opportunity for "toil and trouble" until it is past.

Yet, the psalm is not merely a pessimistic lamentation about life's brevity. It is also an earnest prayer for divine mercy and grace. The poet petitions God to "teach us to count our days," accepting our mortality with a healthy realism, and in that way "we may gain a wise heart" (verse 12). Just as God has decreed that humans "turn" back to dust, so the psalmist cries to God to "turn" and show compassion (verse 13). He asks that God's "steadfast love" bring satisfaction and joy to our daily lives, even as they are marked by fragility and affliction (verses 14–15). As we seek the Lord's deliverance, the psalmist trusts that God can redeem the days and years of our affliction, for it is only God's grace that can give our lives hope.

Although God has set the limits of human life, our lives have purpose when they are joined to God's work and "glorious power." The psalmist prays that "the favor of the Lord our God be upon us," blessing our years with joy and giving success to the work of our hands (verses 16–17). In praying this psalm, we ask God to penetrate our brief lives with the light of eternity. With the presence of his faithful love, a light will shine on the passing of our days, and what seems not to make sense will acquire meaning, transforming dust into rejoicing. God is our eternal home, still abiding with us, redeeming our time, blessing our lives with joy, and prospering the work of our hands.

Reflection and discussion

- Do I consider this psalm to be pessimistic, realistic, or encouraging?

- What is the wisdom to be gained by acknowledging the brevity of life?

- What gives purpose and meaning to "the works of our hands," the endeavors of daily life?

Prayer

O God, our help in ages past, our hope for years to come, a thousand ages in thy sight are like an evening gone, short as the watch that ends the night before the rising sun. Be our guard while troubles last and our eternal home.

It is good to give thanks to the Lord, to sing praises to your name, O Most High; to declare your steadfast love in the morning, and your faithfulness by night. PSALM 92:1–2

The Lord Reigns Over the Wicked and the Righteous

PSALM 92

1 *It is good to give thanks to the Lord,*
to sing praises to your name, O Most High;
2 *to declare your steadfast love in the morning,*
and your faithfulness by night,
3 *to the music of the lute and the harp,*
to the melody of the lyre.
4 *For you, O Lord, have made me glad by your work;*
at the works of your hands I sing for joy.

5 *How great are your works, O Lord!*
Your thoughts are very deep!
6 *The dullard cannot know,*
the stupid cannot understand this:
7 *though the wicked sprout like grass*
and all evildoers flourish,
they are doomed to destruction forever,
8 *but you, O Lord, are on high forever.*
9 *For your enemies, O Lord,*
for your enemies shall perish;
all evildoers shall be scattered.

10 *But you have exalted my horn like that of the wild ox;*
you have poured over me fresh oil.
11 *My eyes have seen the downfall of my enemies;*
my ears have heard the doom of my evil assailants.

12 *The righteous flourish like the palm tree,*
and grow like a cedar in Lebanon.
13 *They are planted in the house of the Lord;*
they flourish in the courts of our God.
14 *In old age they still produce fruit;*
they are always green and full of sap,
15 *showing that the Lord is upright;*
he is my rock, and there is no unrighteousness in him.

PSALM 93

1 *The Lord is king, he is robed in majesty;*
the Lord is robed, he is girded with strength.
He has established the world; it shall never be moved;
2 *your throne is established from of old;*
you are from everlasting.

3 *The floods have lifted up, O Lord,*
the floods have lifted up their voice;
the floods lift up their roaring.
4 *More majestic than the thunders of mighty waters,*
more majestic than the waves of the sea,
majestic on high is the Lord!

5 *Your decrees are very sure;*
holiness befits your house,
O Lord, forevermore.

Addressing God as "Most High," Psalm 92 begins with thanksgiving and praise for God's "steadfast love in the morning" and his "faithfulness by night" (92:1–2). Echoing the time of the temple's morning and evening offering, and then pointing to the music of the lute, harp, and lyre, affirms the liturgical nature of this psalm (92:3). The impulse to worship God arises from the joy and gladness the psalmist feels at God's "works" (92:4).

The psalm draws a parallel between God's great "works" and God's deep "thoughts," the labors and the intentions of God in the world (92:5). God's designs are "deep" not only because they are profound but also because they are hidden from the ordinary view of the insipid and senseless (92:6). Although it seems that the evildoers prosper and enjoy success on many fronts, they will perish and be scattered (92:7–9). While the wicked are destined for "destruction forever," the Lord reigns "on high forever." Focusing on the apparent achievements of the evildoers prevents most people from seeing the depth of God's designs or the height of God's exalted position.

The psalmist allies himself with the righteous, declaring that God has given him strength and refreshment (92:10–11). Like the strength of the wild ox that is concentrated in its death-dealing horn, he has been given the strength to overcome his enemies. And like the oil that brings renewal to a warrior exhausted in battle, he has been given refreshment to continue the fight. Because God has ministered to his needs, the psalmist sees that his enemies are fleeing, and he hears their panic as his assailants are defeated.

In contrast to the inevitable downfall of the wicked, the righteous are destined to flourish (92:12–15). Like palms trees and cedars of Lebanon—a sharp contrast to the wicked that sprout like grass—their growth extends to a long life, enduring and bearing fruit, "always green and full of sap." As with any plants, the growth of the palms and cedars is the result of where they are transplanted: here it is the temple, "the house of the Lord" and "the courts of our God"—a carefully chosen location where they may thrive. The psalmist concludes with his personal testimony to God as upright and righteous, a solid, unmoving rock.

Proclaiming God's indisputable kingship over all creation, Psalm 93 describes God as "robed in majesty" and "girded with strength" (93:1). God has firmly established the earth because the Lord's rule is firm and unmoving (93:2). Yet, the movement of the psalm is vigorous, like the rushing and roaring waters of which it speaks. The roaring floods, mighty waters, and pounding waves of the sea express the chaotic forces that constantly threaten God's rule (93:3–4). Yet, the Lord sustains the world because he reigns "majestic on high," above the threatening waters.

This exalted king has condescended to dwell in the temple, at the very heart of his people with whom he has made a firm, unchanging covenant (93:5). The Lord who has always reigned from heaven's highest throne—"your throne is established from of old; you are from everlasting"—now reigns on his earthly throne from the ark of the covenant "forevermore." The psalm instills confidence and hope in those who feel insecure and afraid of being overwhelmed by the impending forces of chaos and the storms of history.

Reflection and discussion

- How can I remain fresh and green, continuing to flourish and produce fruit?

- Why do the roaring floods, mighty waters, and pounding waves express those forces that continually threaten the world and that must always be contained by God?

- What message of hope do these psalms offer to me?

Prayer

O God Most High, I give you thanks and sing praises to your name. Although it seems that evildoers prosper and enjoy much success, I know that your purposes are hidden and deep. Help me to trust in you and live always with hope.

Light dawns for the righteous, and joy for the upright in heart.
Rejoice in the Lord, O you righteous, and give thanks to his holy name!
PSALM 97:11–12

The Divine King Reigns in Holy Splendor

PSALM 96

1*O sing to the Lord a new song;*
sing to the Lord, all the earth.
2*Sing to the Lord, bless his name;*
tell of his salvation from day to day.
3*Declare his glory among the nations,*
his marvelous works among all the peoples.
4*For great is the Lord, and greatly to be praised;*
he is to be revered above all gods.
5*For all the gods of the peoples are idols,*
but the Lord made the heavens.
6*Honor and majesty are before him;*
strength and beauty are in his sanctuary.

7*Ascribe to the Lord, O families of the peoples,*
ascribe to the Lord glory and strength.
8*Ascribe to the Lord the glory due his name;*
bring an offering, and come into his courts.
9*Worship the Lord in holy splendor;*
tremble before him, all the earth.

10*Say among the nations, "The Lord is king!*
The world is firmly established; it shall never be moved.

He will judge the peoples with equity."
11 *Let the heavens be glad, and let the earth rejoice;*
let the sea roar, and all that fills it;
12 *let the field exult, and everything in it.*
Then shall all the trees of the forest sing for joy
13 *before the Lord; for he is coming,*
for he is coming to judge the earth.
He will judge the world with righteousness,
and the peoples with his truth.

PSALM 97

1 *The Lord is king! Let the earth rejoice;*
let the many coastlands be glad!
2 *Clouds and thick darkness are all around him;*
righteousness and justice are the foundation of his throne.
3 *Fire goes before him,*
and consumes his adversaries on every side.
4 *His lightnings light up the world;*
the earth sees and trembles.
5 *The mountains melt like wax before the Lord,*
before the Lord of all the earth.

6 *The heavens proclaim his righteousness;*
and all the peoples behold his glory.
7 *All worshipers of images are put to shame,*
those who make their boast in worthless idols;
all gods bow down before him.
8 *Zion hears and is glad,*
and the towns of Judah rejoice,
because of your judgments, O God.
9 *For you, O Lord, are most high over all the earth;*
you are exalted far above all gods.

10 *The Lord loves those who hate evil;*
he guards the lives of his faithful;

he rescues them from the hand of the wicked.
11*Light dawns for the righteous,*
and joy for the upright in heart.
12*Rejoice in the Lord, O you righteous,*
and give thanks to his holy name!

These two psalms, like Psalm 93, proclaim that "The Lord is king." These enthronement psalms praise God who reigns over the whole world and governs human history. God's people chanted these psalms regularly as they celebrated God's royal rule during their liturgical worship in the temple.

Psalm 96 begins with calls to praise God (96:1–3). The imperatives are universal in scope, addressed to the peoples of "all the earth." They implore the hearers to sing of God's salvation, his glory, and his marvelous works "among the nations." The whole cosmos reverberates with praise.

The psalm then declares the reasons for the praise (verses 4–5). The Lord is great, worthy to be praised, and revered above all would-be gods or above whatever people strive for, trust in, or worship. "For all the gods of the peoples are idols"—a word that means something like "weakness" or "uselessness." In contrast, "the Lord made the heavens." Although most ancient peoples worshiped the heavenly bodies, God's worthiness to be praised lies in his work as the Creator of all the heavens and the earth. Therefore, all the attributes of divine kingship can be ascribed to God: honor, majesty, strength, beauty, and especially glory (verses 6–9). The "families of the peoples" are invited to "bring an offering, and come into his courts." The courts of the temple were regarded as the courts of the king's royal palace, so bringing an "offering" was not only a liturgical sacrifice but also a political tribute to the divine king. In a sacred ritual, the visiting peoples must bow down in worship before the Lord.

The final section of the psalm specifies the content of the message the congregation must announce among the nations: "the Lord is king," and he reigns over all (verses 10–13). This divine king has firmly established the world with an order in both nature and society that can be trusted. The same Lord who has created the world also will come to judge the world with equity, righteousness, and truth. All the earth can look backward to creation and forward to judgment with confident trust because the Lord reigns.

Because we mistakenly think that divine judgment will be a day of gloom and doom, it might seem strange to us that the impending judgment of God is described here as a cause for rejoicing. But God's judging the world with equity, righteousness, and truth means restoring the world to order and harmony. As God sets things right, the world is restored. So, not only do the people sing praise, but the heavens are glad and the earth rejoices. Everything in creation is joyful, each in its own way: the sea and all its creatures roar, the fields and all the creatures within it exult, and "all the trees of the forest sing for joy." This symphony of creation shows the natural connectedness of all the elements of the created world. The social order of humanity and the created order of nature are intertwined in harmony and peace, a state called throughout the biblical literature "the kingdom of God."

Psalm 97 continues with similar praise, "The Lord is king! Let the earth rejoice," dramatically expressing God's royal authority (97:1–6). As the royal power of human kings is often described as filling the kingdom and its conquered territories, the glory of God fills the cosmos. The "coastlands" are all those places that must be reached by ship—every land in which people are known to exist. Unlike any human king, God's arrival at his throne room fills the world with storm clouds, darkness, lightning, and quaking. Righteousness and justice undergird his reign. Mountains, the most solid reality in creation, melt like wax in the fire because of God's presence. His adversaries give way before his consuming power, while the peoples of the earth behold his glory.

There are two responses to the entry of the divine king (97:7–9). On the one hand, worshipers of idols are shamed and defeated; on the other, those who come to worship the Lord at Zion joyfully raise a hymn of praise. All the would-be gods of the idolaters bow down before the one God, while God's faithful revel in his judgments. Finally, the psalm describes the features of those who await the divine king: they hate evil; they are faithful, righteous, and upright of heart; they rejoice in the Lord and give God thanks (97:10–12). When God's kingdom comes and the Lord reigns supreme, all evil will be defeated, and God's faithful will know eternal joy.

Reflection and discussion

- Why is God's final judgment of the world a cause for rejoicing?

- In what ways does human worship of God parallel the worship of God's other creatures?

- What should I do as I await the coming of God's kingdom?

Prayer

Royal Lord, all creation rightly gives you praise. May my song resound with the heavens and the earth. I await your judgment with joyful anticipation and hope for the coming of your kingdom.

Sing praises to the Lord with the lyre, with the lyre and the sound of melody. With trumpets and the sound of the horn make a joyful noise before the King, the Lord. PSALM 98:5–6

Sing Praises to the Lord of All the Earth

PSALM 98

1 *O sing to the Lord a new song,*
for he has done marvelous things.
His right hand and his holy arm
have gotten him victory.
2 *The Lord has made known his victory;*
he has revealed his vindication in the sight of the nations.
3 *He has remembered his steadfast love and faithfulness*
to the house of Israel.
All the ends of the earth have seen
the victory of our God.

4 *Make a joyful noise to the Lord, all the earth;*
break forth into joyous song and sing praises.
5 *Sing praises to the Lord with the lyre,*
with the lyre and the sound of melody.
6 *With trumpets and the sound of the horn*
make a joyful noise before the King, the Lord.

7 *Let the sea roar, and all that fills it;*
the world and those who live in it.

8 *Let the floods clap their hands;*
let the hills sing together for joy
9 *at the presence of the Lord, for he is coming*
to judge the earth.
He will judge the world with righteousness,
and the peoples with equity.

PSALM 99

1 *The Lord is king; let the peoples tremble!*
He sits enthroned upon the cherubim; let the earth quake!
2 *The Lord is great in Zion;*
he is exalted over all the peoples.
3 *Let them praise your great and awesome name.*
Holy is he!
4 *Mighty King, lover of justice,*
you have established equity;
you have executed justice
and righteousness in Jacob.
5 *Extol the Lord our God;*
worship at his footstool.
Holy is he!

6 *Moses and Aaron were among his priests,*
Samuel also was among those who called on his name.
They cried to the Lord, and he answered them.
7 *He spoke to them in the pillar of cloud;*
they kept his decrees,
and the statutes that he gave them.

8 *O Lord our God, you answered them;*
you were a forgiving God to them,
but an avenger of their wrongdoings.
9 *Extol the Lord our God,*
and worship at his holy mountain;
for the Lord our God is holy.

PSALM 100

1*Make a joyful noise to the Lord, all the earth.*
2*Worship the Lord with gladness;*
come into his presence with singing.

3*Know that the Lord is God.*
It is he that made us, and we are his;
we are his people, and the sheep of his pasture.

4*Enter his gates with thanksgiving,*
and his courts with praise.
Give thanks to him, bless his name.

5*For the Lord is good;*
his steadfast love endures forever,
and his faithfulness to all generations.

These first two psalms conclude the psalter's collection of enthronement psalms, proclaiming that the Lord is king. Since God has created and redeemed his people, he is worthy of our worship. Despite the disasters of sin throughout history, God still reigns over all and will make things right again. But these psalms declare that our praise is more than words lifted heavenward. Our praise must be lived out in faithfulness and obedient trust. The third psalm is an expression of pure praise to God. These three psalms were all composed for those going up to Zion to worship God in the temple.

Psalm 98 begins by calling worshipers to "sing to the Lord a new song" for all the "marvelous things" God has done and the "victory" he has won through his great power (98:1–3). Yet, these saving deeds were not only for Israel's sake; rather, they were revealed "in the sight of the nations." Whether it be Israel's liberation from Egypt, the conquest of the land, the rescue from Assyria, or the deliverance from Babylon, these are divine manifestations "all the ends of the earth have seen."

The next call to praise the Lord is an extended invitation addressed to the whole world. "All the earth" is invited to "make a joyful noise," to "break forth into joyous song," and to "sing praises to the Lord" (98:4–6). Praises are sung to the accompaniment of the “lyre,” which creates the “melody” of the songs. The “trumpet” is a straight metal instrument; the “horn” is the natural horn of a ram or goat. These create a “joyful noise” but not a melody.

The psalm finally turns to the entire creation to join in the praise (98:7–9). The sea, the world, rivers, and hills—this cosmic assembly—“roar,” “clap their hands,” and “sing together for joy.” The universe is united in one purpose: to exalt the divine king, who is “coming to judge the earth.” The great hope of creation is that God will “judge the world with righteousness, and the peoples with equity,” so that the Lord will reestablish the original harmony of creation and bring about a kingdom of justice and peace. Already now the creation breaks forth in anticipatory praise of that great day to come.

Psalm 99 announces again, “The Lord is king,” invisibly enthroned above the outstretched wings of the cherubim atop the ark of the covenant (99:1–2). In response, the peoples of other nations tremble and the earth quakes. For the Lord is enthroned not only over Israel, but “he is exalted over all the peoples.” Yet, the other nations not only fear him but are invited to participate in praising the “great and awesome name” of God as he is revealed through the people of Israel (99:3).

The second section highlights the justice and the resulting good order brought to Israel by their mighty King (99:4–5). The gods of other peoples tended to boast of building projects, military victories, and empires, but the Lord of Israel has established equity, justice, and righteousness. While God is the cause of these social virtues, Israel’s human kings are regularly praised or condemned for the ways they tend to God’s laws, especially as they regard the poor, the marginalized, widows, and orphans.

The final verses review Israel’s acts of faithfulness to God in past ages—namely, during the times of Moses, Aaron, and Samuel (99:6–8). These figures illustrate the dialogical relationship between the Lord and his people: they “called on his name,” and “he answered them.” God’s answering them shows itself in his decrees and statutes as well as in his forgiveness and expiation of their wrongs. Truly the Lord is not just a lawgiver but a God who listens. His justice is not executed with legalistic grimness; rather, it is responsive to human intercession and needs.

The psalm’s refrain is the thrice-repeated “Holy is he!” dividing each stanza and culminating in the extended finale: “For the Lord our God is holy” (99:3,

5, 9). In ancient Israel, to speak of something or someone as "holy" was to designate it as set apart from everyday actions, reserved for sacred use, and accessed through the mediation of ritual actions. God's people must worship their holy God at "his holy mountain," the temple at Zion, the sacred space at the heart of the world where the Lord chose to dwell among humanity.

Psalm 100 consists of alternating calls to praise the Lord (100:1–2, 4) and reasons for praising the Lord (100:3, 5). It is addressed to "all the earth," calling all people to make a joyful noise, worship the Lord, come into his presence, know that the Lord is God, enter his gates, give thanks to him, and bless his name. All are invited to join the liturgical procession and offer exuberant praise of God in the temple. For the Lord is our maker, shepherd, and provider. We belong to him and we need him. Essentially, we come before our God because he is good, steadfastly loving, and constantly faithful.

Reflection and discussion

- What kinds of music and instruments do I use to give praise to God?

- What does it mean to me that I am called to holiness?

- How do I acquire the freedom to live my life more joyfully?

Prayer

Holy, holy, holy, Lord our God, your justice, mercy, and covenant love extend to all the earth. May I praise you with my lips and worship you with joy, for you are my creator, shepherd, and redeemer.

I will look with favor on the faithful in the land, so that they may live with me; whoever walks in the way that is blameless shall minister to me. PSALM 101:6

The Leader's Desire for Integrity of Heart

PSALM 101

1 *I will sing of loyalty and of justice;*
to you, O Lord, I will sing.
2 *I will study the way that is blameless.*
When shall I attain it?

I will walk with integrity of heart
within my house;
3 *I will not set before my eyes*
anything that is base.

I hate the work of those who fall away;
it shall not cling to me.
4 *Perverseness of heart shall be far from me;*
I will know nothing of evil.

5 *One who secretly slanders a neighbor*
I will destroy.
A haughty look and an arrogant heart
I will not tolerate.

6 *I will look with favor on the faithful in the land,*
so that they may live with me;
whoever walks in the way that is blameless
shall minister to me.

7 *No one who practices deceit*
shall remain in my house;
no one who utters lies
shall continue in my presence.

8 *Morning by morning I will destroy*
all the wicked in the land,
cutting off all evildoers
from the city of the Lord.

This psalm is traditionally understood as the commitment of David and the kings of his lineage to the righteous conduct that ought to belong to God's anointed ones. It begins with praise of God's loyalty and justice, the foundation of Israel's monarchy (verse 1). Only these divine gifts enable the king to seek to attain "the way that is blameless" (verse 2). The rest of the psalm develops the king's pursuit of this way, supporting those in his realm who practice it and opposing those who do not.

The king seeks to conduct his reign with "integrity of heart," pursuing choices and actions that are consistent with his dependence on the Lord's loyalty and justice. In contrast, the king seeks to keep away any "perverseness of heart," avoiding conduct that is inconsistent with these divine gifts or lacking coherence with his inner commitment (verse 4). This inward perversity is demonstrated by evil, slander, "a haughty look and an arrogant heart" (verse 5). This emphasis on the heart makes it clear that the king's commitment is not simply to do what is legal and oppose those who do wrong. The psalm is a commitment to develop character, those habits of the heart out of which good conduct emerges. Through the example of the monarch's own life and the influence of his authority, the king vows to establish his reign to reflect the character of the Lord.

In this regard, the king promises to "look with favor on the faithful in the land," and those who live blamelessly will serve as his royal ministers (verse

6). Contrarily, no one "who practices deceit" or "who utters lies" will live in his presence (verse 7). Those who are wicked and all evildoers will be expelled from Jerusalem, "the city of the Lord" (verse 8). Those who wish to be loyal to God must avoid participation in evil company and in the deeds they practice. God's expectations, then, are exemplified in two character profiles: the way of the righteous and the way of the wicked.

The psalm teaches that it is not enough for those who lead and those who are led to live by regulations and legal codes. Whether it be the king in Israel or another leader, it is the character of the leader and of those governed that determines the quality of a nation or community. Conduct depends on character, and character is shaped by ultimate commitments. Ideal leaders must model their authority on God's governance of the world. They must govern with moral integrity and a resolute commitment to justice.

Reflection and discussion

- Why are qualities of the heart and noble character so critical to good governance?

- What are the behaviors that demonstrate poor character and lack of commitment to virtues?

- In what ways does this psalm challenge me to better leadership in my family, work, or community?

Prayer

Just and loyal God, you teach those anointed for service to live lives of integrity. Keep me free from slander, deceit, and lies, and give me integrity of heart so that I may be an example to those entrusted to me.

O grant us help against the foe, for human help is worthless. With God we shall do valiantly; it is he who will tread down our foes. PSALM 108:12–13

Singing with Confidence in God's Promises

PSALM 108

1 *My heart is steadfast, O God, my heart is steadfast;*
I will sing and make melody.
Awake, my soul!
2 *Awake, O harp and lyre!*
I will awake the dawn.
3 *I will give thanks to you, O Lord, among the peoples,*
and I will sing praises to you among the nations.
4 *For your steadfast love is higher than the heavens,*
and your faithfulness reaches to the clouds.

5 *Be exalted, O God, above the heavens,*
and let your glory be over all the earth.
6 *Give victory with your right hand, and answer me,*
so that those whom you love may be rescued.

7 *God has promised in his sanctuary:*
"With exultation I will divide up Shechem,
and portion out the Vale of Succoth.
8 *Gilead is mine; Manasseh is mine;*
Ephraim is my helmet;
Judah is my scepter.
9 *Moab is my washbasin;*
on Edom I hurl my shoe;
over Philistia I shout in triumph."

[10]*Who will bring me to the fortified city?*
Who will lead me to Edom?
[11]*Have you not rejected us, O God?*
You do not go out, O God, with our armies.
[12]*O grant us help against the foe,*
for human help is worthless.
[13]*With God we shall do valiantly;*
it is he who will tread down our foes.

If the opening verses of this psalm sound familiar (verses 1–5), it is because they are the closing verses of Psalm 57. Likewise, the second half of this psalm (verses 6–13) forms the closing verses of Psalm 60. By fusing together these two psalm fragments, a new psalm arises. The new psalm is something more than the mere juxtaposition of two preexisting passages. Rather than beginning with a nightmarish scenario and pleading for God's help, as in the opening passages of Psalms 57 and 60, this psalm starts by launching into an exuberant hymn of praise to "awake the dawn," and it ends with confidence in God's help.

This psalm provides us with a model of how the tradition of Israel often reused more ancient texts to illuminate new situations. The living word of God, animated by the divine Spirit, may be recontextualized and actualized in many situations different from the original. The Christian tradition has often done the same, using more ancient passages and combining them in new ways, in the New Testament and in the Christian liturgy.

The psalm opens with a joyful morning song. The psalmist summons his soul, his musical instruments, and a voice filled with song and declares, "Awake, my soul! Awake, O harp and lyre! I will awake the dawn" (verses 1–2). All are ready to participate in the song of thanksgiving and praise to God for his twin attributes, "steadfast love" and "faithfulness"—those divine qualities that have sustained God's people in covenant for generation after generation (verses 3–4). The individual singer is presented within an international and universal context, as he prays that God be exalted "above the heavens" and that God's glory cover "over all the earth" (verse 5).

The second half of the psalm pleads for God to answer the singer's prayers for victory and rescue for God's beloved people (verse 6). Amid Israel's anguish, as they feel the absence and rejection of God, the psalmist prays with hope. This confidence arises with an oracle of the Lord, promised to his people in the temple (verses 7–9). This divine oracle declares the Lord's dominion over the cities, tribes, and territories that composed the kingdom of David. It even claims God's rights over three subjugated enemies: neighboring Moab in the southeast, Edom in the south, and coastal Philistia. In contrast to the noble imagery used to describe the tribes of Israel, "helmet" and "scepter," these conquered enemies are associated with the "washbasin" one uses for bathing, the dirty "shoe" that must be cleaned after battle, and the cry of subjection after conquest. The metaphors express humiliation and servitude.

The psalm concludes as a corporate prayer for God's help (verses 10–13). Seeking God's protection and lamenting that God no longer accompanies the armies of his people, the psalm turns to trust. It ends in an assertion of confidence in God's help against the foes, knowing that "human help is worthless." but "with God we shall do valiantly." Because the Lord reigns, there is nothing to fear. Even in the darkest times, there is always a superior plan that governs history. God will always reveal himself anew to sustain and guide his people.

Reflection and discussion

- Why is Scripture often applied in new ways, apart from its original context?

- What is an example of an ancient biblical text being used in the new context of the Christian liturgy?

Prayer

O God my strength, who guides me through the passages of life, enable me to trust in you when I feel that you are absent or have abandoned me. Help me realize that human help is worthless without your gracious presence.

SUGGESTIONS FOR FACILITATORS, GROUP SESSION 5

1. Welcome group members and ask if anyone has any questions, announcements, or requests.

2. You may want to pray this prayer as a group:
   O God, you are our help in ages past, our hope for years to come. How great are your works, how deep are your thoughts. Guide us through the passages of life, help us realize that human help is worthless without your gracious presence, and enable us to trust in you when we feel that you are absent or have abandoned us. Keep us free from slander, deceit, and lies, and give us integrity of heart so that we may be examples to those entrusted to us. May we await your judgment with joyful anticipation and hope for the coming of your kingdom.

3. Ask one or both of the following questions:
   - What most intrigued you from this week's study?
   - What makes you want to know and understand more of God's word?

4. Discuss lessons 19 through 24. Choose one or more of the questions for reflection and discussion from each lesson to talk over as a group.

5. Ask the group members to name one thing they have most appreciated about the way the group has worked during this Bible study. Ask group members to discuss any changes they might suggest in the way the group works in future studies.

6. Invite group members to complete lessons 25 through 30 on their own during the six days before the next meeting. They should write out their own answers to the questions as preparation for next week's session.

7. Ask group members to name ways that their study of these Psalms is enriching their practice of prayer.

8. Conclude by praying aloud together the prayer at the end of one of the lessons discussed. You may want to conclude the prayer by asking members to voice prayers of thanksgiving.

Blessed is the one who comes in the name of the Lord. We bless you from the house of the Lord. The Lord is God, and he has given us light. PSALM 118:26–27

Thanksgiving for God's Faithful Love

PSALM 117

1 *Praise the Lord, all you nations!*
Extol him, all you peoples!
2 *For great is his steadfast love toward us,*
and the faithfulness of the Lord endures forever.
Praise the Lord!

PSALM 118

1 *O give thanks to the Lord, for he is good;*
his steadfast love endures forever!

2 *Let Israel say,*
"His steadfast love endures forever."
3 *Let the house of Aaron say,*
"His steadfast love endures forever."
4 *Let those who fear the Lord say,*
"His steadfast love endures forever."

5 *Out of my distress I called on the Lord;*
the Lord answered me and set me in a broad place.

6 With the Lord on my side I do not fear.
What can mortals do to me?
7 The Lord is on my side to help me;
I shall look in triumph on those who hate me.
8 It is better to take refuge in the Lord
than to put confidence in mortals.
9 It is better to take refuge in the Lord
than to put confidence in princes.

10 All nations surrounded me;
in the name of the Lord I cut them off!
11 They surrounded me, surrounded me on every side;
in the name of the Lord I cut them off!
12 They surrounded me like bees;
they blazed like a fire of thorns;
in the name of the Lord I cut them off!
13 I was pushed hard, so that I was falling,
but the Lord helped me.
14 The Lord is my strength and my might;
he has become my salvation.

15 There are glad songs of victory in the tents of the righteous:
"The right hand of the Lord does valiantly;
16 the right hand of the Lord is exalted;
the right hand of the Lord does valiantly."
17 I shall not die, but I shall live,
and recount the deeds of the Lord.
18 The Lord has punished me severely,
but he did not give me over to death.

19 Open to me the gates of righteousness,
that I may enter through them
and give thanks to the Lord.

20 This is the gate of the Lord;
the righteous shall enter through it.

21 *I thank you that you have answered me*
and have become my salvation.
22 *The stone that the builders rejected*
has become the chief cornerstone.
23 *This is the Lord's doing;*
it is marvelous in our eyes.
24 *This is the day that the Lord has made;*
let us rejoice and be glad in it.
25 *Save us, we beseech you, O Lord!*
O Lord, we beseech you, give us success!

26 *Blessed is the one who comes in the name of the Lord.*
We bless you from the house of the Lord.
27 *The Lord is God,*
and he has given us light.
Bind the festal procession with branches,
up to the horns of the altar.

28 *You are my God, and I will give thanks to you;*
you are my God, I will extol you.

29 *O give thanks to the Lord, for he is good,*
for his steadfast love endures forever.

Although Psalm 117 is the shortest of the psalms, the scope of its praise is vast. Its call to worship God includes the whole world, the nations and their many peoples (117:1). The universal Lord merits universal worship. Praise of God is not complete until it draws every people on the globe to joyfully recognize that the Lord is the one and only God, the centering focus of all seeking and truth. The call to praise the Lord envisions a unity beyond divisions, clarity beyond confusion, and peace beyond contention.

This psalm is just long enough to include both elements of a psalm of praise: the call to praise in the first verse, and the reasons for that praise in the second verse. The basis of worshiping God is his "steadfast love" and his "faithfulness," the vocabulary that expresses the central attributes of God in the saving covenant (117:2). Despite his people's infidelity, God will never fail or abandon his people. The steadfast love and faithfulness of God is unconditional, tireless, and never ending.

Psalm 118 concludes the collection of six psalms called the Hallel (Pss 113—118), songs of praise that were sung in connection with the Passover and other festivals, remembering God's deliverance of his people from the bondage of Egypt. These were the psalms sung by Jesus and his disciples at the end of the Passover supper. Psalm 117 is the briefest and Psalm 118 is the lengthiest, summarizing the themes of each of the others in the Hallel collection.

The psalm is a thanksgiving liturgy which celebrates deliverance, framed within choral praise of God's "steadfast love" (118:1–4, 29). The alternation of individual and choral voices, repetitions, refrains, and references to procession, temple gates, and altar, indicate communal worship.

The singular voice in the psalm—"Out of my distress I called on the Lord…With the Lord on my side I do not fear"—speaks on behalf of the congregation (118:5–9). The speaker's voice represents the communal experience of God's people. In recounting his victory over enemies, he gives all credit to the powerful help of the Lord, who frees him from fear and gives him confidence that he will prevail over his foes. With "the Lord on my side," he declares, he will "take refuge in the Lord" and triumph. Despite the fierceness of their attack—"They surrounded me like bees; they blazed like a fire of thorns"—he conquered them decisively—"In the name of the Lord I cut them off!"—through the Lord's saving help (118:10–14).

In response to this narrative of a decisive triumph, the Lord's people shout "glad songs of victory," attributing their success to "the right hand of the Lord," the active intervention of God (118:15–18). Knowing that God intended his suffering for the good and did not give him over to death, the speaker vows to recount the mighty deeds of the Lord's salvation.

Reaching the gates of the temple, the speaker requests admission in the name of the congregation to "give thanks to the Lord" by offering a thanksgiving sacrifice (118:19–29). This entrance liturgy consists of antiphonal call and response. The speaker pleads, "Open to me the gates of righteousness," and the choir responds, "This is the gate of the Lord; the righteous shall enter through it." The speaker then addresses God: "I thank you that you have answered me and have become my salvation," to which the choir responds with praise to God for reversing human expectations with marvelous, divine solutions: "The stone that the builders rejected has become the chief cornerstone." What humans reject, God makes the pivotal center of his saving plan. The festive procession continues through the temple courts, right up to "the horns of the altar."

The passion accounts of the four gospels all quote verses 25–26 in connection with Jesus' triumphal procession through Jerusalem and into the courts of the temple. As Jesus enters the city for his final Passover, the people cry out, Hosannah, "Save us, we beseech you, O Lord!" Jesus also quotes the axiom of the rejected stone becoming the cornerstone as a summary of God's plan for his final messianic mission. We can hear the words of the speaker in this psalm as the words of Jesus himself, affirming his trust as he faces his impending trial and suffering. The early Christians read the psalm in liturgy as a prophetic promise of the Messiah's ultimate vindication by God, who raised him from the dead and established him as the cornerstone of the new temple.

Reflection and discussion

- What indicates that Psalm 118 is a procession and communal liturgy?

- How does verse 22 describe the mission of Jesus in God's plan for salvation? What difference does it make to read Psalm 118 in the voice of Christ?

Prayer

You are my God, I give thanks to you, for you have saved me in my distress and given me victory over my foes. O give thanks to the Lord, for he is good, for his steadfast love endures forever.

Let me hear of your steadfast love in the morning, for in you I put my trust. Teach me the way I should go, for to you I lift up my soul. PSALM 143:8

Answer Me and Do Not Hide Your Face

PSALM 143

1 *Hear my prayer, O Lord;*
give ear to my supplications in your faithfulness;
answer me in your righteousness.
2 *Do not enter into judgment with your servant,*
for no one living is righteous before you.

3 *For the enemy has pursued me,*
crushing my life to the ground,
making me sit in darkness like those long dead.
4 *Therefore my spirit faints within me;*
my heart within me is appalled.

5 *I remember the days of old,*
I think about all your deeds,
I meditate on the works of your hands.
6 *I stretch out my hands to you;*
my soul thirsts for you like a parched land. Selah

7 *Answer me quickly, O Lord;*
my spirit fails.
Do not hide your face from me,
or I shall be like those who go down to the Pit.
8 *Let me hear of your steadfast love in the morning,*
for in you I put my trust.

Teach me the way I should go,
for to you I lift up my soul.

9*Save me, O Lord, from my enemies;*
I have fled to you for refuge.
10*Teach me to do your will,*
for you are my God.
Let your good spirit lead me
on a level path.

11*For your name's sake, O Lord, preserve my life.*
In your righteousness bring me out of trouble.
12*In your steadfast love cut off my enemies,*
and destroy all my adversaries,
for I am your servant.

The psalm expresses a prayer for deliverance from an enemy's pursuit. Beginning with a series of pleas to God—"Hear my prayer," "give ear to my supplications," and "answer me"—the person in prayer appeals to God's faithfulness and righteousness (verse 1). God's righteousness is his divine will and saving work to set things right, despite all that denies and perverts God's will and work in the world. The psalmist prays not to be put on trial or brought to judgment before God (verse 2). The psalmist's reason is unlike most other prayers for help in the Bible. Usually, the one pleading to God states that he doesn't deserve to be in the situation, that he wants to be judged according to his righteousness and integrity. However, here the psalmist states emphatically, "No one living is righteous before you." The prayer appeals to the general predicament in which all people stand: our human unworthiness and unrighteousness before God.

The trouble described in the psalm arises because of an enemy, a mortal foe whose work leads to darkness and death (verses 3–4). The assaults of the adversary create a feeling of being completely alienated from others in the community. This lack of human support makes for a spirit that is faint and a heart that is desolate. Left with the memories of God's saving deeds among his people in the past, the psalmist longs for God's response (verses 5–6). Meditating on the work of God's "hands," he stretches out his own hands to God. The soul yearning for God is like "parched land" thirsty for quenching rains.

Following the transitional "Selah," the second half of the prayer expresses the human longing for God's help in a sustained series of pleas: answer me, do not hide from me, let me hear, teach me, save me, lead me, preserve me, bring me out of trouble, cut off my enemies, destroy my adversaries (verses 7–12). Each petition to God is supported by a motive for the plea, expressing the perilous condition of the psalmist and confidence in his relationship with God. Without God's help, he will be "like those who go down to the Pit," at the threshold of the grave. Fearing the dark night of the Pit, the poet longs to experience God's "steadfast love in the morning." With each new dawn, his hope is renewed as he prays, "In you I put my trust."

This prayer for deliverance gives every indication of a particularly intimate relationship between the psalmist and God. The words arise from deep within the psalmist and are freighted with deep emotion. He flees to God for refuge from the foes, and he seeks God's instructions so that he may know and follow God's will, mentioning that the agent of that guidance is God's "spirit." What is evident throughout the prayer is the abandonment of the "servant" into God's hands. He is confident of God's response, ready and attentive to the divine voice, as he closes with the signature, "I am your servant."

Reflection and discussion

- What seem to be the enemies that threaten the psalmist's life and well-being? What motivates the psalmist in his distress?

- How does the psalm feel different when I pray it in the first person, rather than considering the situation of the original psalmist?

Prayer

Lord our God, faithful and righteous, hear my plea and protect me from my enemies. Teach me your holy will and give me the insight to trust in your way. May your Holy Spirit lead me to follow as your servant.

The Lord sets the prisoners free; the Lord opens the eyes of the blind. The Lord lifts up those who are bowed down; the Lord loves the righteous. PSALM 146:7–8

Praising the Lord Who Keeps Faith Forever

PSALM 146

1 *Praise the Lord!*
Praise the Lord, O my soul!
2 *I will praise the Lord as long as I live;*
I will sing praises to my God all my life long.

3 *Do not put your trust in princes,*
in mortals, in whom there is no help.
4 *When their breath departs, they return to the earth;*
on that very day their plans perish.

5 *Happy are those whose help is the God of Jacob,*
whose hope is in the Lord their God,
6 *who made heaven and earth,*
the sea, and all that is in them;
who keeps faith forever;
7 *who executes justice for the oppressed;*
who gives food to the hungry.

The Lord sets the prisoners free;
8 *the Lord opens the eyes of the blind.*
The Lord lifts up those who are bowed down;
the Lord loves the righteous.

9 *The Lord watches over the strangers;*
he upholds the orphan and the widow,
but the way of the wicked he brings to ruin.

10 *The Lord will reign forever,*
your God, O Zion, for all generations.
Praise the Lord!

Psalm 146 introduces a collection of five psalms that form a finale of praise to God. Each of these (Pss 146—150) begins and ends with the Hebrew word *Halleluiah*, a plural imperative call to "Praise the Lord!" The praise is eternal and cosmic in its scope, including all creation. This last assembly of psalms leads to Psalm 150, a glorious hymn of pure praise.

Following the opening call for all to "Praise the Lord," the singular voice of the psalmist invokes his own soul, his whole being, to give praise and sing to the Lord. He then vows to praise God throughout his life, for as long as life may last (verses 1–2). The speaker here is probably a liturgical leader, since the remainder of the psalm goes on to offer instruction in wisdom for the community.

The first part of the instruction is a negative in form: "Do not put your trust in princes" (verses 3–4). The psalmist warns the people not to trust in human leaders to save them from their difficulties, for at their death all their projects and plans die with them. Then the hopes of all who placed their trust in them are dashed. Israel's experience with their human leaders is reflected in this wisdom. Of course, the instruction does not claim that leaders are unnecessary or not useful, but it warns against trusting them for salvation. Hope based on what is transient will certainly result in disappointment.

The positive side of this instruction takes the form of a long beatitude: "Happy are those whose help is the God of Jacob" (verses 5–9). The God revealed to Israel's ancestors is a leader whose reign is everlasting. Those who put their hope in the Lord will never be dismayed. He is the sole creator of the sky, land, and sea, and of all the creatures that inhabit them. Because he is the creator and ruler of all that exists, he is able to save the world. We are able to trust God completely because of a primary character trait: he "keeps faith forever." The psalmist then recites all the divine activities by which the Lord keeps faith.

The Lord's help comes especially to those who find no help in humanity: the oppressed, the hungry, the prisoners, the blind, those bowed down, the righteous, the stranger, the widow and orphan. The Lord's help in each case heals the damage done to his human creatures. He helps those who cannot help themselves. As the creator of all, God not only helps the helpless, but he also judges the ways of the wicked, bringing to ruin the abusive power of those who damage or neglect the lost and forsaken ones whom he loves. If the Lord did not vindicate the righteous and thwart the wicked, he would not be keeping faith.

The closing verse addresses Zion directly: those who experience the reign of God on earth (verse 10). A characteristic of the Lord's kingship is caring for the powerless and marginalized, a responsibility that human leaders generally fail to fulfill. This description of God's character cannot be sung without thinking of the down-to-earth salvation brought to the world by Jesus. He showed in his preaching and healing that the kingdom of God belongs to the poor and lowly, those whom human authorities neglect to help. This singular beatitude is expanded by Jesus in his Sermon on the Mount. Through the saving ministry of Jesus, God has decisively ranked himself on the side of the victims, the oppressed, and the lost. The path of trust means sharing his choices and character. It means embracing the one who saves us already and who will judge our lives in their completeness on our decisions to serve him in the hungry, the thirsty, the foreigner, the naked, the sick, and the prisoner.

Reflection and discussion

- Why is adoration and praise the highest form of prayer?

- What is the problem with putting trust and hope in human institutions and leaders?

Prayer

Lord God, I praise you now and forever. Turn my mind and heart to you, so that I may conform my desires to your will, my values to what you treasure, and my support to those in need.

Praise the Lord, O Jerusalem! Praise your God, O Zion! For he strengthens the bars of your gates; he blesses your children within you. PSALM 147:12–13

Praise to the God of Jerusalem and of the Cosmos

PSALM 147

1 *Praise the Lord!*
How good it is to sing praises to our God;
for he is gracious, and a song of praise is fitting.
2 *The Lord builds up Jerusalem;*
he gathers the outcasts of Israel.
3 *He heals the brokenhearted,*
and binds up their wounds.
4 *He determines the number of the stars;*
he gives to all of them their names.
5 *Great is our Lord, and abundant in power;*
his understanding is beyond measure.
6 *The Lord lifts up the downtrodden;*
he casts the wicked to the ground.

7 *Sing to the Lord with thanksgiving;*
make melody to our God on the lyre.
8 *He covers the heavens with clouds,*
prepares rain for the earth,
makes grass grow on the hills.

9He gives to the animals their food,
and to the young ravens when they cry.
10His delight is not in the strength of the horse,
nor his pleasure in the speed of a runner;
11but the Lord takes pleasure in those who fear him,
in those who hope in his steadfast love.

12Praise the Lord, O Jerusalem!
Praise your God, O Zion!
13For he strengthens the bars of your gates;
he blesses your children within you.
14He grants peace within your borders;
he fills you with the finest of wheat.
15He sends out his command to the earth;
his word runs swiftly.
16He gives snow like wool;
he scatters frost like ashes.
17He hurls down hail like crumbs—
who can stand before his cold?
18He sends out his word, and melts them;
he makes his wind blow, and the waters flow.
19He declares his word to Jacob,
his statutes and ordinances to Israel.
20He has not dealt thus with any other nation;
they do not know his ordinances.
Praise the Lord!

This psalm is divided into three sections, each introduced by a call to the assembly to give praise to the Lord. The first invocation exclaims "how good it is to sing praises to our God" because God is "gracious" and it is "fitting" to give him praise (verse 1). The second call to praise urges the congregation to "sing to the Lord with thanksgiving," with attention to its musical accompaniment on the lyre (verse 7). The third invocation specifies the people of Jerusalem as those called to give praise to God (verse 12).

Following each of the calls to praise, the psalmist voices the reasons why it is right to give God praise. In the first and third section, God is honored as the one who restores the city of Jerusalem. Not only does God build up the ruined structures of the city and bring back those who were exiled, he also heals the anguish and grief of those whose hope is being revived (verses 2–3). As the people of the city give God praise, he strengthens Jerusalem's defenses from attack, brings blessings and peace to its inhabitants, and fills them with nourishing wheat (verses 13–14).

Each of the three sections then offers praise of God for his mastery over the cosmos. First, God "determines the number of the stars" and "gives to all of them their names," which exemplifies that God is "abundant in power" yet also "understanding" beyond measure (verses 4–5). Although the transition from the city to the cosmos might seem abrupt, it is joined by the providence of God over both creation and his beloved people. As God counts the stars in the sky and kindly names each one, God also powerfully guides the history of his people and tenderly binds their wounds. Second, God covers the sky with clouds, supplies rain to make the grass grow, and feeds the grazing animals and the helpless young ravens (verses 8–9). His mighty power and limitless understanding have established an ecological system to provide for the needs of all. In the third section, God sends out his word to bring snow, frost, and hail, chilling his creation, then he sends out his word again to melt the ice and snow, making gentle breezes and flowing waters (verses 15–18).

At the end of each of the three sections, the psalmist highlights the particularities of God's favor. At the end of the first section, the psalmist proclaims, "The Lord lifts up the downtrodden; he casts the wicked to the ground," emphasizing God's care for the lowly and his fury at evil (verse 6). The conclusion of the second section declares that what brings God delight is not the natural strength of his creatures—neither a horse's might nor a runner's speed—but rather those who exhibit a rightful fear of his majesty and those who hope in his faithful love (verses 10–11). And finally, at the end of the third section, the psalmist highlights how God has declared the word of his revelation to his own chosen people, joining them in covenant unlike any other people (verses 19–20).

While each of these three sections would be a meaningful prayer in its own right, the abundant praise that results from their combination is far more profound. The song is skillfully woven in so that it joins the diverse threads of God's ways in the cosmos and with his own people. The complete psalm causes us to marvel at the Lord's providence over all of creation and at his unfailing and faithful love for his people in Jerusalem.

Reflection and discussion

- In verses 2–3, God is described as a builder and a healer. What other images of God are used in the psalm?

- Because God both counts and names the stars, he is described by the psalmist as "abundant in power" and "understanding beyond measure" (verses 4–5). In what other ways is God shown to be both powerful and understanding?

- In verses 15–18, the psalmist describes how God's word causes the transition from winter to spring. How have you witnessed God effecting a transition for you?

Prayer

How good it is to sing praises to you, O Lord. As the power of your word causes changes in the cosmos, so you bring comfort and healing to your people. May I fear your awesome might and hope in your steadfast love.

Young men and women alike, old and young together!
Let them praise the name of the Lord, for his name alone is exalted;
his glory is above earth and heaven. PSALM 148:12–13

Heaven and Earth Sing Praise to God

PSALM 148

1 *Praise the Lord!*
Praise the Lord from the heavens;
praise him in the heights!
2 *Praise him, all his angels;*
praise him, all his host!

3 *Praise him, sun and moon;*
praise him, all you shining stars!
4 *Praise him, you highest heavens,*
and you waters above the heavens!

5 *Let them praise the name of the Lord,*
for he commanded and they were created.
6 *He established them forever and ever;*
he fixed their bounds, which cannot be passed.

7 *Praise the Lord from the earth,*
you sea monsters and all deeps,
8 *fire and hail, snow and frost,*
stormy wind fulfilling his command!

9 Mountains and all hills,
fruit trees and all cedars!
10 Wild animals and all cattle,
creeping things and flying birds!

11 Kings of the earth and all peoples,
princes and all rulers of the earth!
12 Young men and women alike,
old and young together!

13 Let them praise the name of the Lord,
for his name alone is exalted;
his glory is above earth and heaven.
14 He has raised up a horn for his people,
praise for all his faithful,
for the people of Israel who are close to him.
Praise the Lord!

As one of the five Halleluiah psalms, this song not only opens and closes with "Praise the Lord," but once the cry of praise is uttered, it repeats the cry over and over, inviting all creation to join in the praise of God. This cosmic worship is composed of two great choirs: one "from the heavens" (verses 1–6) and the other "from the earth" (verses 7–14). In this ancient vision of creation, the heavens and the earth are the two realms that constitute the cosmos. Each section concludes with an invitation to each choir to give glory to God: "Let them praise the name of the Lord" (verses 5, 13).

Representatives from every part of the created world are summoned to sing God's praises. The heavenly creatures include the angels, sun, moon, stars, and clouds (verses 2–4). Their grandeur proclaims the glory of God, and they respond to their call to praise God by shining forth in all their radiance. The reason for their praise is profoundly simple: God has created them and continues to govern them (verses 5–6).

The earthly creatures include the creatures of the sea and the ocean depths (verse 7). They encompass the various meteorological phenomena that affect the earth: lightning, hail, snow, frost, winds, and storms (verse 8). The panorama of creation incorporates the mountains, hills, fruit trees, cedars, wild and domestic animals, creatures that crawl on the earth, and birds that fly in the air (verses 9–10). Many creatures in the roll call are designated by the word "all," indicating that the list is inclusive, representing everything that exists. The psalm recruits the entire realm of creation to offer praise to God.

Finally, human beings are the last to enter this picture of total praise (verses 11–12). There is no designation of man and woman as superior to the other creatures. They are simply one section of a universal chorus. Designated as royal rulers and peoples, men and women, old and young, all are equal in God's sight despite office, gender, or age. Like that of the heavens, the reason for the earth's praise is also profound and clear: "His name alone is exalted: his glory is above heaven and earth" (verse 13).

Those who are close to God, "the people of Israel," experience power and purpose when they join in the universal praise of God (verse 14). Just as the snowflake and the fruit tree show forth praise of God by being what they are as God's creatures, so the people of Israel, having been made what they are now by God, show forth God's praise by being who they are, the nation joined in covenant with God.

From the perspective of faith, praise of God is at the heart of the universe and is the core purpose of every created being. As human beings, sometimes we limit our praise to our own immediate circumstances and to what God has done specifically for us. But the psalms broaden our perspective as they testify to the praiseworthiness of the Lord in every moment by every creature. Situating ourselves within the vastness of all creation's worship, we discover within ourselves a reverent wonder for who God truly is. We realize the narrow vision of a culture that looks only to human profits from the earth, and we understand more fully the marvelous dignity of being a creature of God.

Reflection and discussion

- How many times does the psalm include the word "all"? Why does the psalmist use this designation so often?

- In what way does this cosmic chorus broaden my perspective in praising God?

- What wisdom does this psalm offer for my responsibility to care for God's creation?

Prayer

Maker of heaven and earth, in the wonder of the natural world, I can sense how beautiful must be the unseen world you have made. May I always give you praise and thanks, along with the angels in the heights and all the creatures of the sky, earth, and sea.

Let them praise his name with dancing, making melody to him with tambourine and lyre. For the Lord takes pleasure in his people; he adorns the humble with victory.

PSALM 149:3–4

Praising God with Song, Dance, and Musical Instruments

PSALM 149

1 *Praise the Lord!*
Sing to the Lord a new song,
his praise in the assembly of the faithful.
2 *Let Israel be glad in its Maker;*
let the children of Zion rejoice in their King.
3 *Let them praise his name with dancing,*
making melody to him with tambourine and lyre.
4 *For the Lord takes pleasure in his people;*
he adorns the humble with victory.
5 *Let the faithful exult in glory;*
let them sing for joy on their couches.
6 *Let the high praises of God be in their throats*
and two-edged swords in their hands,
7 *to execute vengeance on the nations*
and punishment on the peoples,
8 *to bind their kings with fetters*
and their nobles with chains of iron,

9 *to execute on them the judgment decreed.*
This is glory for all his faithful ones.
Praise the Lord!

PSALM 150

1 *Praise the Lord!*
Praise God in his sanctuary;
praise him in his mighty firmament!
2 *Praise him for his mighty deeds;*
praise him according to his surpassing greatness!

3 *Praise him with trumpet sound;*
praise him with lute and harp!
4 *Praise him with tambourine and dance;*
praise him with strings and pipe!
5 *Praise him with clanging cymbals;*
praise him with loud clashing cymbals!
6 *Let everything that breathes praise the Lord!*
Praise the Lord!

The Psalter concludes with hymns of praise. Psalm 149 issues the invitation to "Praise the Lord" and to "Sing to the Lord a new song." The key word of the psalm seems to be the "faithful" ones (*hasidim,* in Hebrew), those who loyally express steadfast love for God (149:1, 5, 9). The Lord is depicted as both their Maker and their King, forming Israel as a nation and ruling over them, and they are invited to praise God joyfully with dancing and musical instruments (149:2–3). The call to praise is followed by a twofold reason to praise God: one for God's benefit: "the Lord takes pleasure in his people"; and the other for how God benefits his people: "he adorns the humble with victory" (149:4).

A second summons to praise invites the "faithful" ones to "exult in glory" and "sing for joy," with "high praises of God" in their throats and "two-edged swords in their hands" (149:5–6). It seems that the psalm has taken a turn from praise of God to militancy against others. The call to praise is followed by a series of infinities which define a course of action including the execution of vengeance, punishment, and judgment (149:7–9). The Lord's victory will bring "glory for all his faithful ones."

The joining of this combative rhetoric with a song of praise suggests that the militancy should be read as spiritual warfare. Whether the original context of the psalm spoke of violent combat or figurative battle, the later Jewish and Christian traditions prayed this psalm as spiritual warfare against the powerful forces arrayed against God's kingdom. God's faithful ones sing praise to God in the morning and then go forth into the world filled with evil and injustice. Because they are allied with their Maker and King, victory over evil is certain as the faithful ones engage in the daily struggle.

For those who follow the Messiah, the psalm shows us that combat and invocation, battle and blessing, are inseparable. Paul's writings help us understand this type of warfare: "For our struggle is not against enemies of blood and flesh, but against the rulers, against the authorities, against the cosmic powers of this present darkness, against the spiritual forces of evil in the heavenly places" (Eph 6:12). For this battle we must put on "the whole armor of God," which includes "the shield of faith," "the helmet of salvation, and the sword of the Spirit, which is the word of God" (Eph 6:13–17).

Psalm 150 sets a seal on the Psalter, the hymnbook of God's people. This is a hymn of pure praise; the imperative "Praise the Lord!" rings in every line. Its few verses detail the where, why, how, and who of this praise to God.

The "where," the location of God's praise, is described as "his sanctuary," the holy shrine or temple where he dwells on earth, and "his mighty firmament," the dome in the heavens above which his throne is established (150:1). Worshippers on earth and in heaven are invited to join their praise to God. The "why" of the praise is described as God's "mighty deeds" and his "surpassing greatness"—nothing more specific than this (150:2). Actually, everything that the previous 149 psalms have affirmed about God offers the reason and the content for this praise.

The "how" of praise seems to incorporate every known musical instrument that human genius has invented (150:3–5). The trumpet was played by priests; the lute, harp, and cymbals were played by Levites; and the tambourine, strings, and pipe were played by anyone. Both music within the temple liturgy and music played in festive celebrations were forms of praise to God.

And, finally, the "who" of praise includes "everything that breathes," all living creatures (150:6). The community that praises God includes not just Israelite, not just human, and not just earthly. All creation—visible and invisible, earthly and heavenly, timely and eternal—adores God with unencumbered praise.

Reflection and discussion

- What could singing to God add to my personal prayer?

- In what sense do I praise God while I am engaged in some form of warfare?

- How do these psalms teach me to offer praise that is pleasing to God?

Prayer

My Maker and King, I sing your praises as you dwell in heaven and on earth. With songs of praise on my lips and the sword of your word in my hand, may I prove myself as your faithful one, seeking your will on earth as it is in heaven.

SUGGESTIONS FOR FACILITATORS, GROUP SESSION 6

1. Welcome group members and make any final announcements or requests.

2. You may want to pray this prayer as a group:
   Lord God, may your people always give you praise, along with the angels in the heights and all the creatures of the sky, earth, and sea. As the power of your word causes changes in the cosmos, you bring comfort and healing to your people. Turn our minds and hearts to you, conform our desires to your will, and match our values to what you treasure. We give you thanks, for you have saved us in distress and given us victory over our foes. O give thanks to the Lord, for he is good, for his steadfast love endures forever.

3. Ask one or both of the following questions:
   - How has this study of the psalms enriched your life?
   - In what way has this study challenged you the most?

4. Discuss lessons 25 through 30. Choose one or more of the questions for reflection and discussion from each lesson to discuss as a group.

5. Ask the group if they would like to study another book in the *Threshold Bible Study* series. Discuss the topic and dates and make a decision among those interested. Ask the group members to suggest people they would like to invite to participate in the next study series.

6. Ask the group to discuss the insights that stand out most from this study over the past six weeks.

7. Conclude by praying aloud the following prayer or another of your own choosing:
   Holy Spirit of the living God, you inspired the writers of the Scriptures and you have guided our study during these weeks. Continue to deepen our love for the word of God in the holy Scriptures and draw us more deeply into the heart of Jesus. We thank you for the confident hope you have placed within us and the gifts that build up the church. Through this study, lead us to worship and witness more fully and fervently, and bless us now and always with the fire of your love.